MODULE SIX

Answer Book

Roy Edwards
Mary Edwards
Alan Ward

Cambridge University Press
Cambridge
New York Port Chester
Melbourne Sydney

Published by the Press Syndicate of the University of Cambridge
The Pitt Building, Trumpington Street, Cambridge CB2 1RP
40 West 20th Street, New York, NY 10011, USA
10 Stamford Road, Oakleigh, Melbourne 3166, Australia

First published 1990

Printed in Great Britain by Scotprint, Musselburgh, Scotland

British Library cataloguing-in-publication data

ISBN 0 521 35832 9

Typeset by Oxprint, Oxford, OX2 6TR

Contents

Number 1

A p. 4

1 3811
2 1823
3 2920
4 1942
5 40
6 400
7 5768

8 244, 344, 444, 544

9 362, 462, 562, 662

10

20	10	20	40	80
100	120	150	110	180

11

100	200	400	400	600
300	500	800	800	600

12

		11	
	6		
			1

13

		5	
	6		
14			

14

		15	
	7		
13			

15 The magic number is 34 for each square.
Each square has been turned through a right angle.
They all use the same numbers.

B p. 6

1 2243
2 1927
3 3141
4 1852
5 2825
6 4300
7 1121
8 1200 (ice skating)
1100 (ice hockey)
2100 (skiing)
800 (curling)
9 skiing, ice skating, ice hockey
10 4400
11 1265 1143 518 396
12 1355 1233 608 486
13 1643
14 1643
Both answers are the same.
15 800
16 2000
17 1900
18 1900

19

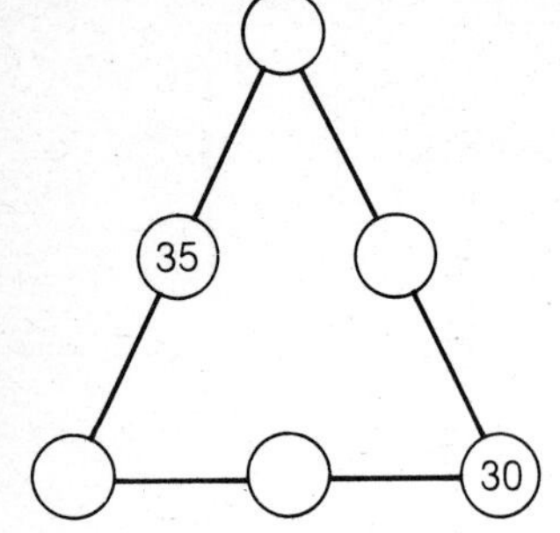

20

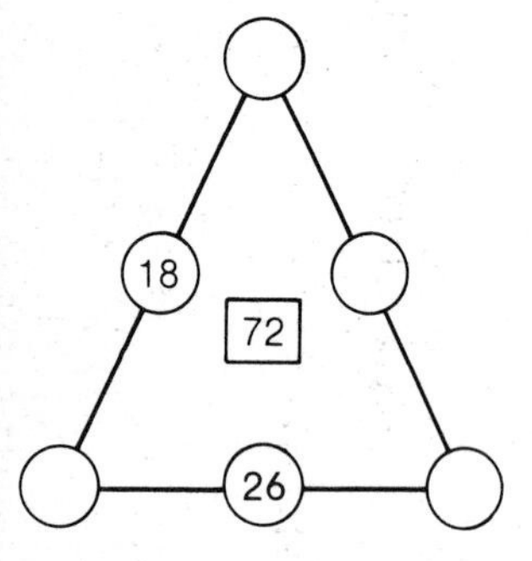

C p. 8

1 1896 1900 1904 1908
1912 — 1920 1924
1928 1932 1936 —
— 1948 1952 1956
1960 1964 1968 1972
1976 1980 1984 1988

2 1992 1996 2000 2004
2008 2012

3 622

Number 2

A p. 9

1 1877 1896 1900 1918
1946 1967

2 1777 1796 1800 1818
1846 1867

3 877 896 900 918 946
967

4 1790 1822
1794 1839

5 1873

6 1957

7 84 years

8 28 years

9 25 years

10 29 years

11 44 years

12 9 years

13 24 years

14 1924 1914 1904

15 1880 1860 1840

16 1923 1918 1913

17 1800

18 1800

19 1900

20 1800

21 1900

22 10 2

23 1000 90

24 900 30

B p. 12

1 1799 1821 1831 1838
1902 1911 1937 1953
(1956)

2 71 years

3 16 years

4 80 years

5 35 years

6 90 years

7 Edward VII

8 George V

9 157 years

10 19th 20th 20th 19th
20th 19th
20th
19th

11 1890 1940 1920 1880
1950 1890
1950
1880

12 1900 1900 1900 1900
2000 1900
1900
1900

13 1000 − 800 = 200
14 900 − 50 = 850

15 90 − 3 = 87
16 1000 − 900 = 100
17 800 − 70 = 730
18 30 − 8 = 22
19 1864
Answer depends on present year.

C p. 14

1 2 **2** 0
3 6 **4** 7
5 1915 → 1910 → 1905 → 1900 → 1895
6 1934 → 1924 → 1914 → 1904 → 1894
7 1942 → 1939 → 1936 → 1933 → 1930

Shape 1

A p. 15

1 2 **2** 4 **3** 3
4 1 **5** 3 **6** 4
7 equilateral triangle square regular pentagon regular hexagon
8 3 4 5 6
9

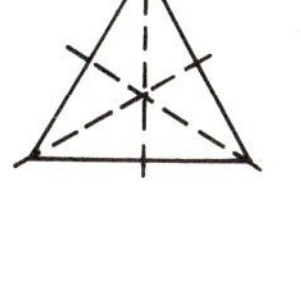
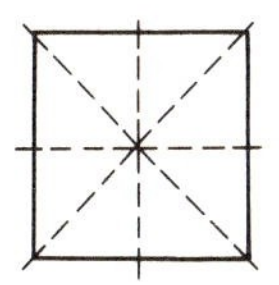
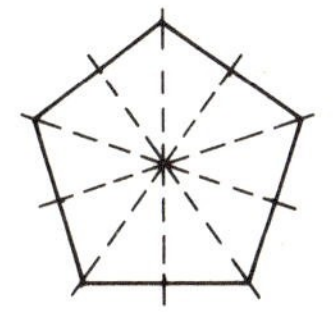
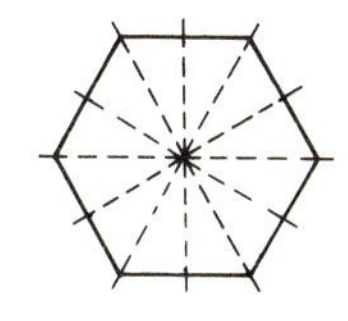

10

shape	△	□	⬠	⬡
number of lines of symmetry	3	4	5	6

11 The number of lines of symmetry is the same as the number of sides and the number of angles.
12 cuboid
13 8 cubes

B p. 17

1 1
2 4
3 1

In the following answers there is a plane that passes through all polyspheres.

4 6 (5+1)
5 4 (3+1)
6 2 (1+1)
7 5 (4+1)
8 5 (4+1)

9 7 (6+1)

10 all cubes

11 Making a bigger cube.

12 There are planes of symmetry across the diagonals which you cannot show by splitting the bigger cube.

13 2

C p. 19

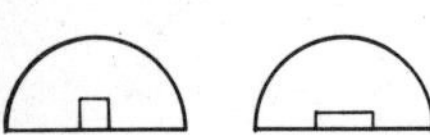

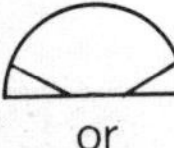

or

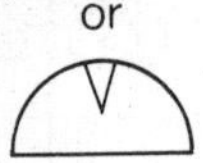

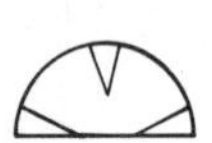

2

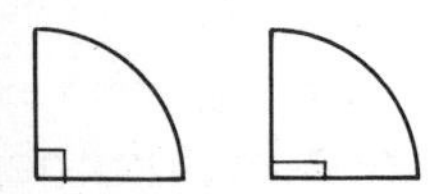

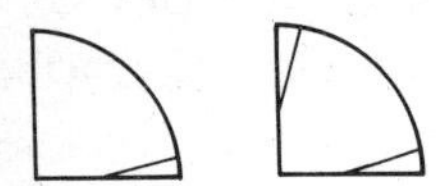

3

		×	×		
	×	×	×	×	
×	×	×	×	×	×
×	×	×	×	×	×
	×	×	×	×	
		×	×		

×	×	×	×	×	×
×	×	•	•	×	×
×	•	×	×	•	×
×	•	×	×	•	×
×	×	•	•	×	×
×	×	×	×	×	×

•	•	⊠	⊗	⊗	⊠	•	•
•	×	⊗	⊠	⊠	⊗	×	•
×	•	⊠	•	•	⊠	•	×
⊗	×	•	⊗	⊗	•	×	⊗
⊗	×	•	⊗	⊗	•	×	⊗
×	•	⊠	•	•	⊠	•	×
•	×	⊗	⊠	⊠	⊗	×	•
•	•	⊠	⊗	⊗	⊠	•	•

Data 1

A p. 20

1 They are not blue and not squares.

2 They are both blue and squares.

3 The white shape is a square but not blue.

4 The triangles are blue but not squares.

5

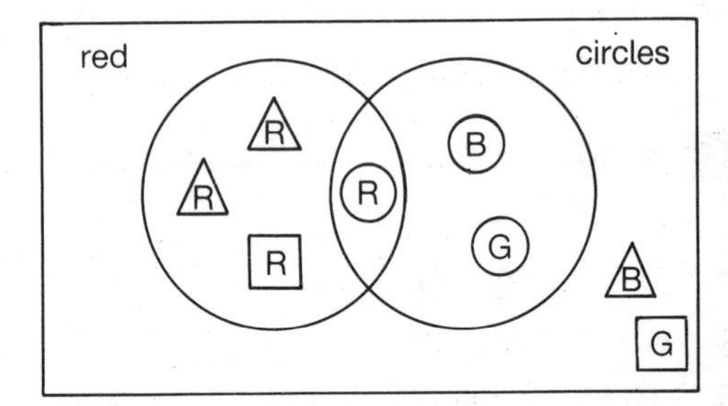

6

△R	Red and not a circle
△R	Red and not a circle
○B	Not red but a circle
□G	Not red and not a circle
□R	Red and not a circle
○G	Not red but a circle
○R	Red and a circle
△B	Not red and not a circle

7 large cube → 6 faces all square
small cube → 6 faces all square
cuboid → 6 faces not all square
triangular prism → not 6 faces, not all square
sphere → not 6 faces, not all square
cuboid → 6 faces not all square
cylinder → not 6 faces, not all square
pyramid → not 6 faces, not all square

8

	Some triangular faces	no triangular faces
Some square corners	triangular prism pyramid	large cube small cube 2 cuboids
no square corners		sphere cylinder

B p. 22

1

squares — blue: B B
squares — not blue: Y G R
not squares — blue: B B
not squares — not blue: R Y

2 Remember, squares are special rectangles.

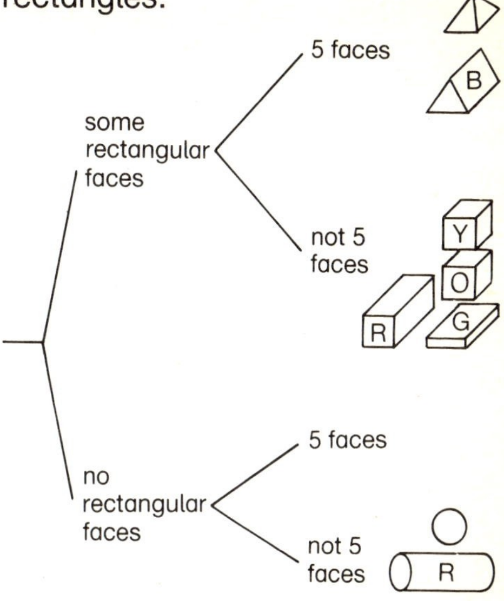

Other ways of recording are possible.

C p. 23

1

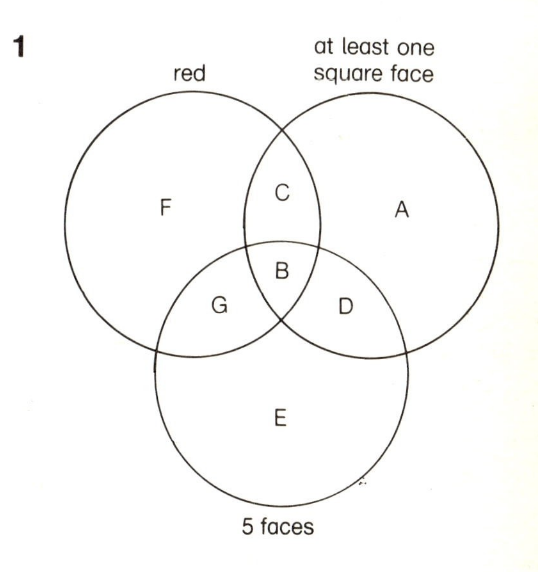

Number 3

A p. 24

1 2 4 6 8 10 12 14 16 18 20
2 26 28 30 32 34 36 38 40 42 44
3 84 86 88 90 92 94 96 98 100 102
4 58 46 100
5 32
6 27
7 23
8 17
9 41
10 43
11 5 10 15 20 25 30 35 40 45 50
12 60 65 70 75 80 85 90 95 100 105
13 125 130 135 140 145 150 155 160 165 170
14 The numbers end in 0 or 5.
15 9
16 12
17 17
18 10
19 16
20 19
21 2
22 5
23 7
24 10
25 13
26 18
27 35 90 160 55
28 90 160

B p. 26

1 3 6 9 12 15 18 21 24 27 30
2 36 39 42 45 48 51 54 57 60 63
3 72 75 78 81 84 87 90 93 96 99
4 11
5 17
6 28
7 13
8 19
9 25
10 3
11 9
12 6
13 12 (1+2 = 3)
14 9
15 15 (1+5 = 6)
16 The sum of the digits is divisible by 3
The sum of the digits add up to 3, 6 or 9

C p. 27

1 9
2 10
3 18
4 17
5 21
6 36
7 9
8 18 → 1 + 8 = 9
9 18 → 1 + 8 = 9
10 18 → 1 + 8 = 9
11 The sum of the digits is 9.

Money 1

A p. 28

1 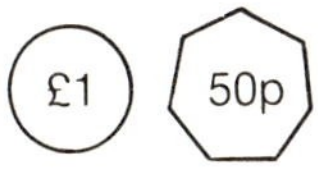 £1 50p

2 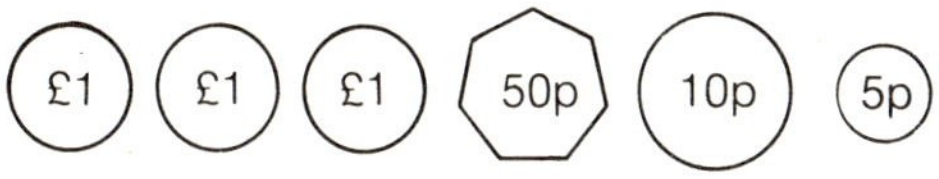 £1 £1 £1 50p 10p 5p

3  £1 50p 20p 20p 5p

4 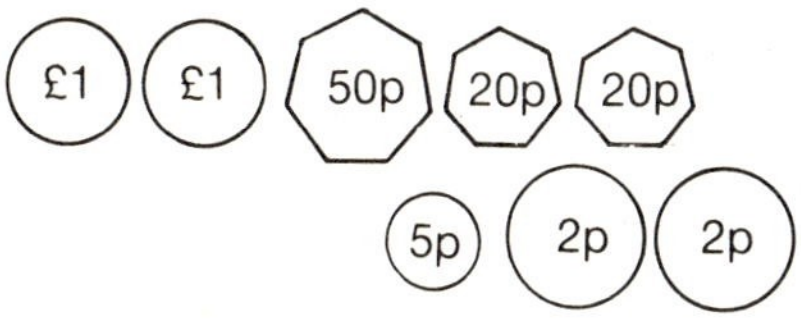 £1 £1 50p 20p 20p 5p 2p 2p

5 £1 £1 50p

6 150p
7 365p
8 195p
9 299p
10 250p
11 495p
12 £3·45
13 £8·60
14 £7·45
15 £4·94
16 £6·25
17 £5·99
18 £8·00

19

David	Jane	Ajit	Naomi
£2·25	£3·50	£6·45	£7·30

20 Ajit Naomi
21 £1·25
22 26p
23 75p
24 £3·31

B p. 30

1 various answers
2 various answers
3 various answers
4 various answers

5

1	2	3
£2·50	£5·00	£7·50

4	5	6
£10·00	£12·50	£15·00

6

1	2	3
£3·25	£6·50	£9·75

4	5	6
£13·00	£16·25	£19·50

7

1	2	3
£3·60	£7·20	£10·80

4	5	6
£14·40	£18·00	£21·60

8

	3.75
	1.06
TOTAL	4.81
TENDERED	5.00
CHANGE	0.19

9

1.99
1.47
0.74
TOTAL 4.20
TENDERED 5.00
CHANGE 0.80

10 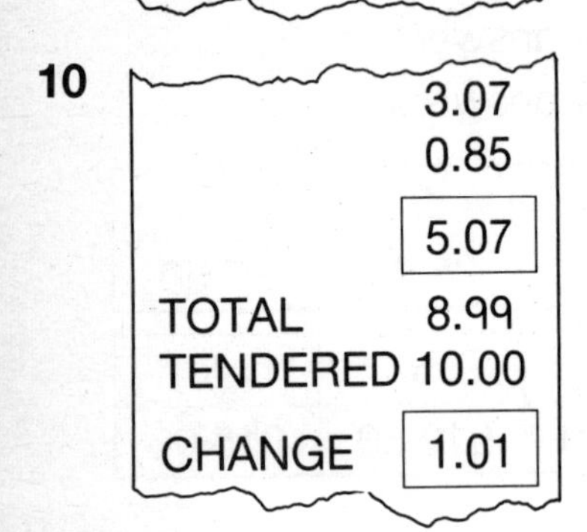

11 £1
12 £3
13 £3
14 £7
15 £2
16 £6
17 £2 + £4 = £6·00 estimate
Exact £6·05
Difference £0·05

Number 4

A p. 33

1 25°C
2 5°C
3 0°C
4 −5°C
5 various answers possible

6 °C
3
2
1
0
−1
−2
−3

B p. 34

1 Winter
2 Newcastle
3 London
4 Glasgow
5 Belfast, Edinburgh, Inverness
6 Jersey
7 Bristol
8 30°C 23°C 21°C 21°C 2°C 0°C −1°C −2°C −3°C −7°C −9°C −15°C
9 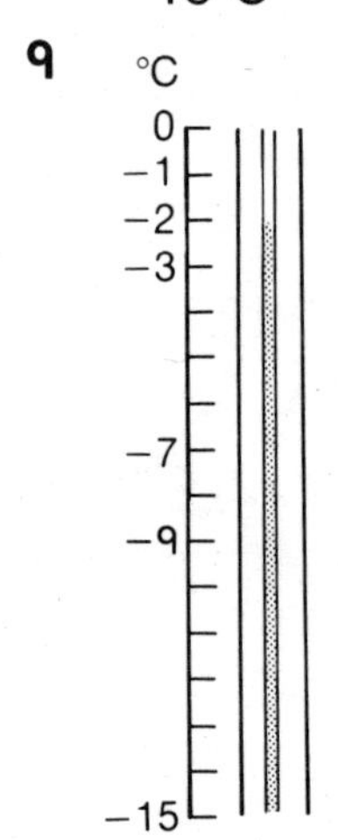

10 Nearer the Equator

C p. 35

1 −17°C
−11°C
−5°C
1°C
7°C
13°C
19°C
25°C

2 Above 4000 m

Probability 1

A p. 36

1–5 Heads and Tails game.

6 Yes. Heads or tails have an equal chance of winning.

7 Either. Both have an equal chance.

8 Dice tally chart

9 Yes. There are six numbers, one on each face.

10–16 Answers may be different for each child.

B p. 39

1–3 Odds and Evens game

4 Yes. There are the same number of ways of throwing an odd number as an even number.

C p. 40

1 3 should win.

2 3 should win.

3 3 should win.

4 No. 2 can only be scored with 1 + 1, 4 only with 2 + 2 but 3 can be scored with 1 + 2 or 2 + 1.

5 No. It is not possible to score less than 1 + 1 = 2.

Number 5

A p. 41

1 $\frac{1}{6}$

2 $\frac{4}{6}$

3

0		
0		

4

0	0	0
0	0	

Other arrangements are possible.

5 $\frac{7}{12}$

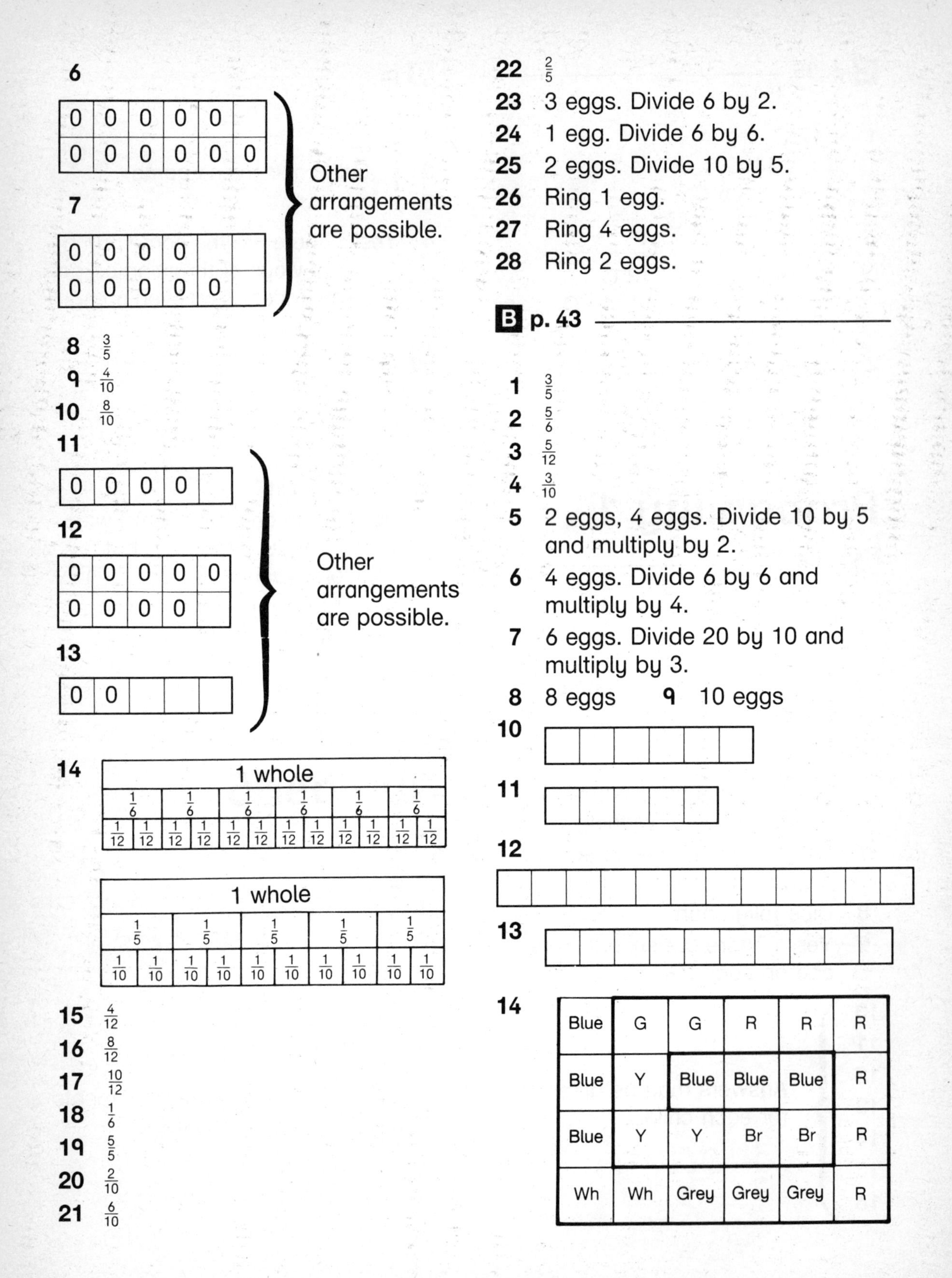

6

0	0	0	0	0	
0	0	0	0	0	0

7

0	0	0	0		
0	0	0	0	0	

Other arrangements are possible.

8 $\frac{3}{5}$

9 $\frac{4}{10}$

10 $\frac{8}{10}$

11

0	0	0	0	

12

0	0	0	0	0
0	0	0	0	

13

0	0			

Other arrangements are possible.

14

1 whole											
$\frac{1}{6}$		$\frac{1}{6}$		$\frac{1}{6}$		$\frac{1}{6}$		$\frac{1}{6}$		$\frac{1}{6}$	
$\frac{1}{12}$	$\frac{1}{12}$	$\frac{1}{12}$	$\frac{1}{12}$	$\frac{1}{12}$	$\frac{1}{12}$	$\frac{1}{12}$	$\frac{1}{12}$	$\frac{1}{12}$	$\frac{1}{12}$	$\frac{1}{12}$	$\frac{1}{12}$

1 whole									
$\frac{1}{5}$		$\frac{1}{5}$		$\frac{1}{5}$		$\frac{1}{5}$		$\frac{1}{5}$	
$\frac{1}{10}$	$\frac{1}{10}$	$\frac{1}{10}$	$\frac{1}{10}$	$\frac{1}{10}$	$\frac{1}{10}$	$\frac{1}{10}$	$\frac{1}{10}$	$\frac{1}{10}$	$\frac{1}{10}$

15 $\frac{4}{12}$

16 $\frac{8}{12}$

17 $\frac{10}{12}$

18 $\frac{1}{6}$

19 $\frac{5}{5}$

20 $\frac{2}{10}$

21 $\frac{6}{10}$

22 $\frac{2}{5}$

23 3 eggs. Divide 6 by 2.

24 1 egg. Divide 6 by 6.

25 2 eggs. Divide 10 by 5.

26 Ring 1 egg.

27 Ring 4 eggs.

28 Ring 2 eggs.

B p. 43

1 $\frac{3}{5}$

2 $\frac{5}{6}$

3 $\frac{5}{12}$

4 $\frac{3}{10}$

5 2 eggs, 4 eggs. Divide 10 by 5 and multiply by 2.

6 4 eggs. Divide 6 by 6 and multiply by 4.

7 6 eggs. Divide 20 by 10 and multiply by 3.

8 8 eggs **9** 10 eggs

10

11

12

13

14

Blue	G	G	R	R	R
Blue	Y	Blue	Blue	Blue	R
Blue	Y	Y	Br	Br	R
Wh	Wh	Grey	Grey	Grey	R

C p. 45

1 $\frac{4}{10}$ $\frac{6}{10}$ $\frac{7}{10}$ $\frac{8}{10}$ $\frac{9}{10}$

2 $\frac{1}{5}$ $\frac{2}{5}$ $\frac{3}{5}$ $\frac{4}{5}$

3 $\frac{1}{6}$ $\frac{2}{6}$ $\frac{4}{6}$ $\frac{5}{6}$

4 $\frac{1}{12}$ $\frac{2}{12}$ $\frac{3}{12}$ $\frac{4}{12}$ $\frac{5}{12}$ $\frac{6}{12}$ $\frac{7}{12}$ $\frac{8}{12}$ $\frac{9}{12}$ $\frac{10}{12}$ $\frac{11}{12}$

Number 6

A p. 46

1

8	24	32	40
2	6	8	10

2

12	28	40	100
3	7	10	25

3 20

4 50

5 65

6 60

7 33

8 9

9 75

10 60

11 95

12 85

13 65

14 45

15

Input	?	Output
1	6	1
2	7	2
4	9	4
5	10	5
3	8	3
7	12	7
6	11	6

16 70

17 90

18 80

19 90

20 100

21 30

22 120

23 210

24 500

B p. 48

1 6

2 11

3 3

4 7

5 2

6 3

7 $\frac{2}{4}$

8 $\frac{4}{8}$

9 $\frac{8}{16}$

10

<table>
<tr><td colspan="8">$\frac{1}{2}$</td><td colspan="8">$\frac{1}{2}$</td></tr>
<tr><td colspan="4">$\frac{1}{4}$</td><td colspan="4">$\frac{1}{4}$</td><td colspan="4">$\frac{1}{4}$</td><td colspan="4">$\frac{1}{4}$</td></tr>
<tr><td colspan="2">$\frac{1}{8}$</td><td colspan="2">$\frac{1}{8}$</td><td colspan="2">$\frac{1}{8}$</td><td colspan="2">$\frac{1}{8}$</td><td colspan="2">$\frac{1}{8}$</td><td colspan="2">$\frac{1}{8}$</td><td colspan="2">$\frac{1}{8}$</td><td colspan="2">$\frac{1}{8}$</td></tr>
<tr><td>$\frac{1}{16}$</td><td>$\frac{1}{16}$</td><td>$\frac{1}{16}$</td><td>$\frac{1}{16}$</td><td>$\frac{1}{16}$</td><td>$\frac{1}{16}$</td><td>$\frac{1}{16}$</td><td>$\frac{1}{16}$</td><td>$\frac{1}{16}$</td><td>$\frac{1}{16}$</td><td>$\frac{1}{16}$</td><td>$\frac{1}{16}$</td><td>$\frac{1}{16}$</td><td>$\frac{1}{16}$</td><td>$\frac{1}{16}$</td><td>$\frac{1}{16}$</td></tr>
</table>

11 $\frac{1}{2} \rightarrow \frac{2}{4} \rightarrow \frac{4}{8} \rightarrow \frac{8}{16}$

12 They are all equal to $\frac{1}{2}$.

13 $\frac{1}{3} \rightarrow \frac{2}{6} \rightarrow \frac{4}{12}$

14 $\frac{2}{3} \rightarrow \frac{4}{6} \rightarrow \frac{8}{12}$

15

Input	Double	Halve	Output
5	10	5	5
7	14	7	7
10	20	10	10
24	48	24	24
35	70	35	35

16 The number stays the same.

17

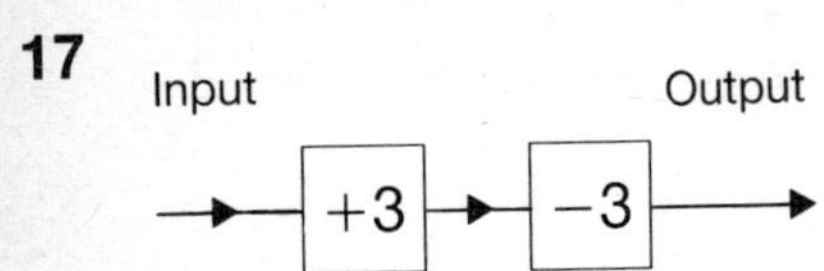

18

Input → −2 → +2 → Output

19

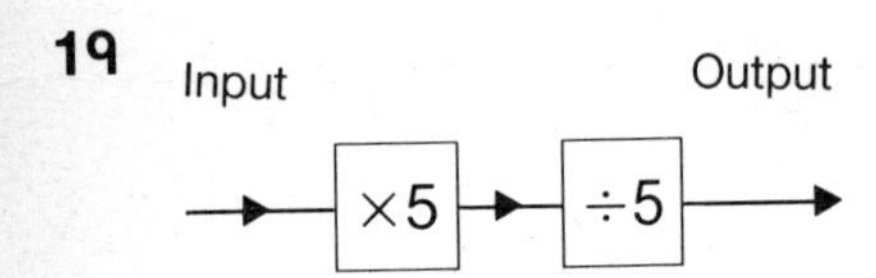

20

Input → ÷2 → ×2 → Output

21

Input	Output
3	5
10	19
21	41
7	13
9	17

22 All the numbers are odd.

23 1

C p. 50

1

Input → ×4 → ×5 → Output

Other answers are possible.

2

Input → ×20 → Output

3

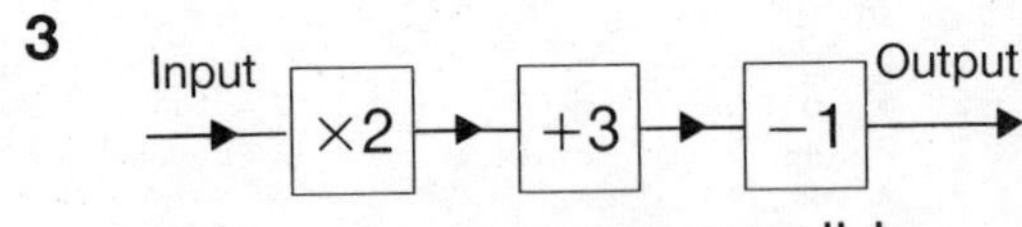

Other answers are possible.

4

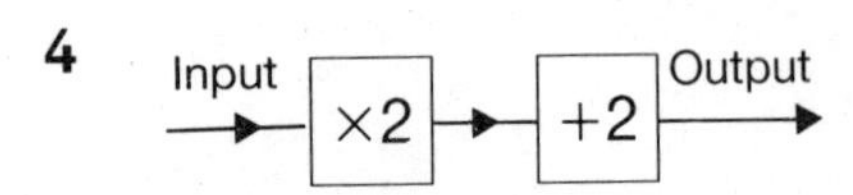

5 3

6 It reverses the number.

7 It outputs the smallest number.

8

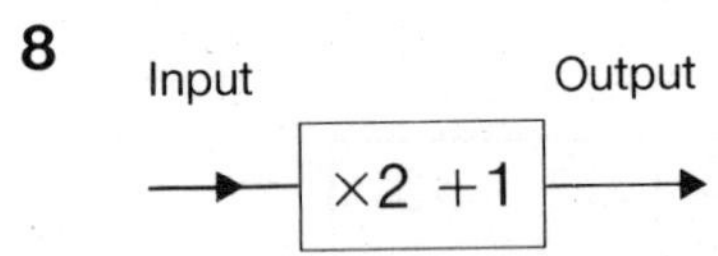

Length 1

A p. 52

1

2 the diameter

3 at the centre

4 the circumference

5 3 cm

6 1 cm

7 2 cm

8 100 cm

9 10 m

10/11

Circle	Radius	Diameter
red	1 cm	2 cm
yellow	2 cm	4 cm
green	3 cm	6 cm
blue	4 cm	8 cm

12 The diameter is double the radius each time.
The radius is half the diameter each time.

B p. 54

2 various answers
3 various answers
4 various answers
5 various answers
6 15
7 32
8 27
9 72 cm
10 90 cm
11 120 cm
12 30
13 40
14 50

C p. 56

1 6 m
2 36 m
3 120 m
4 2 times
5 5 times
6 12 times
7 The small tyre will wear out first. It turns 3 times every time the large wheel turns once. It should wear out 3 times as fast.
8 Tyres on cars with small wheels wear out faster than on cars with larger wheels if they travel the same distance. The smaller wheels turn more times than the larger wheels and therefore have more contact with the road, which wears them out faster.

Weight 1

A p. 57

1 The letter weighs 40 g.
2 The parcel weighs 2 kg 200 g.
3 350 g
4 120 g
5 4 kg 500 g
6 1 kg 500 g
7 Answers depend on the apparatus.
8, 9, 10 } Stretch balance work
11 The scissors stretch the band more because they are heavier than the key.

B p. 59

1 1·300 kg or 1300 g
2 2·800 kg or 2800 g
3 2·100 kg or 2100 g
4 1·900 kg or 1900 g
5 Various graphs are possible.
6, 7, 8, 9 } Answers depend on objects chosen.

C p. 61

1 various answers
2 various answers
3 various answers
4 The number of pages; the size of the pages; the thickness of the paper.

Volume and capacity

A p. 62

1 2000 ml = 2·000 l or 2 l
2 3000 ml = 3·000 l or 3 l
3 2500 ml = 2·500 l
4 1480 ml = 1·480 l
5 160 ml = 0·160 l
6 220 ml = 0·220 l
7 140 ml = 0·140 l
8 450 ml = 0·450 l
9 350 ml = 0·350 l
10 200 ml = 0·200 l
11 open
12 The water level is now at 130 ml.
13 The water level is now at 120 ml.
14 The water level is at 110 ml.
15 I think that 1 centimetre cube will make the water level rise 1 ml.

B p. 64

1–5 Answers depend on the jug and stones chosen.
6 The volume of the stone does not change.

C p. 65

1 Answer depends on cloth chosen.

Time 1

A p. 66

1 8 o'clock
2 11 o'clock
3 4 o'clock
4 Sundials only work when the sun is shining and cannot be used at night.
5 2:21 or 21 minutes past 2
6 6:07 or 7 minutes past 6
7 11:12 or 12 minutes past 11
8 9:03 or 3 minutes past 9
9 10:38 or 38 minutes past 10
10 1:56 or 56 minutes past 1
11 2:48 or 48 minutes past 2
12 4:43 or 43 minutes past 4

B p. 68

1 7
2 9

3 5

4 6

5

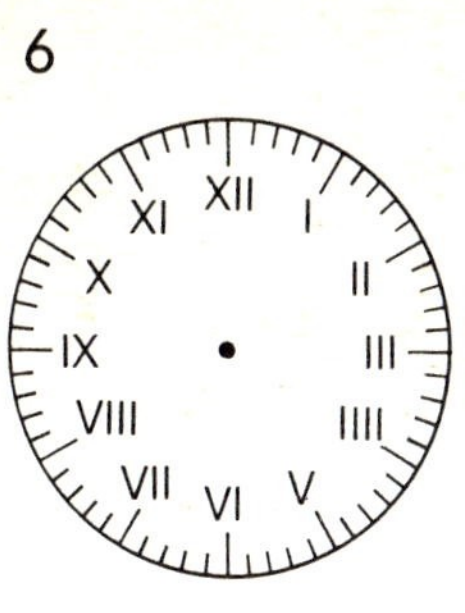

6 12:16

7 10:28

8 2:36

9 9:41

10 2:49

11 4:07

12

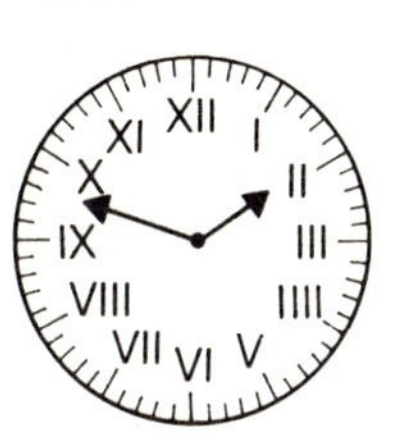

13

14

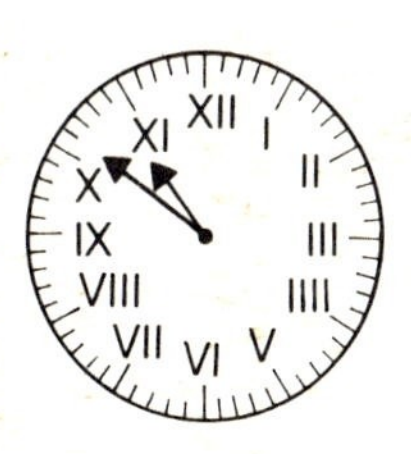

15

16

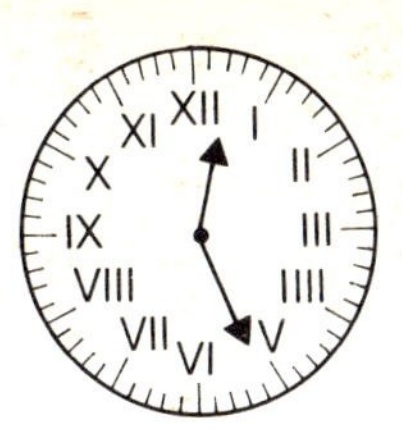

17

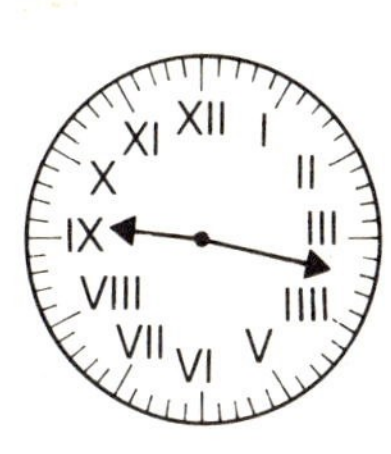

18

Red team	Time	Points
Abida	10 secs	20
Bob	9 secs	35
Total points		55

19

Yellow team	Time	Points
Zoe	8 secs	55
David	14 secs	1
Total points		56

20

Blue team	Time	Points
Susan	12 secs	5
Talika	9 secs	35
Total points		40

21

Green team	Time	Points
Emma	11 secs	10
Ranjit	10 secs	20
Total points		30

22 The Yellow team

C **p. 70**

2 15 seconds approximately. Other answers are possible.

3 40 complete swings approximately. Other answers are possible.

Number 7

A **p. 71**

1 $2 \times 4 = 8$
$4 \times 2 = 8$

2 $8 \times 9 = 72$
$9 \times 8 = 72$

3 $3 \times 4 = 12$
$4 \times 3 = 12$

4 $6 \times 4 = 24$
$4 \times 6 = 24$

5 $4 \times 5 = 20$
$5 \times 4 = 20$

6 $8 \times 7 = 56$
$7 \times 8 = 56$

7 $7 \times 5 = 35$
$5 \times 7 = 35$

8 $10 \times 8 = 80$
$8 \times 10 = 80$

9

X	1	2	3	4	5	6	7	8	9	10
1	1	2	3	4	5	6	7	8	9	10
2	2	4	6	8	10	12	14	16	18	20
3	3	6	9	12	15	18	21	24	27	30
4	4	8	12	16	20	24	28	32	36	40
5	5	10	15	20	25	30	35	40	45	50
6	6	12	18	24	30	36	42	48	54	60
7	7	14	21	28	35	42	49	56	63	70
8	8	16	24	32	40	48	56	64	72	80
9	9	18	27	36	45	54	63	72	81	90
10	10	20	30	40	50	60	70	80	90	100

The pattern is symmetrical about the diagonal line.

10 $21 \times 3 = 63$
$63 \div 3 = 21$

11 $23 \times 2 = 46$
$46 \div 2 = 23$

12 $16 \times 3 = 48$
$48 \div 3 = 16$

13 $32 \times 3 = 96$
$96 \div 3 = 32$

14 $27 \times 2 = 54$
$54 \div 2 = 27$

15 $21 \times 4 = 84$
$84 \div 4 = 21$

16 Each question uses only three numbers.

17 $221 \times 4 = 884$
$884 \div 4 = 221$

18 $117 \times 2 = 234$
$234 \div 2 = 117$

19 $132 \times 3 = 396$
$396 \div 3 = 132$

20 $4 \times 9 = 36$

21 $8 \times 9 = 72$

22 $5 \times 9 = 45$

23 $1 \times 11 = 11$
$2 \times 11 = 22$

$3 \times 11 = 33$

24 $2 \times 11 = 22$
$4 \times 11 = 44$

$6 \times 11 = 66$

25 $1 \times 11 = 11$
$8 \times 11 = 88$

$9 \times 11 = 99$

B p. 73

2

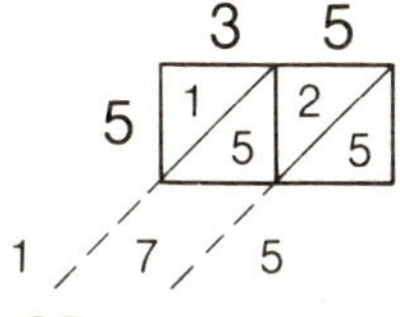

$35 \times 5 = 175$

3

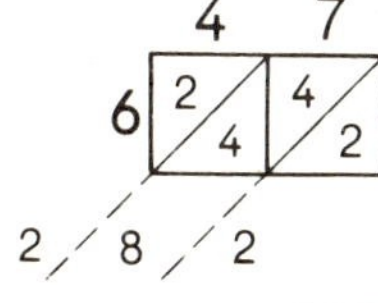

$47 \times 6 = 282$

4

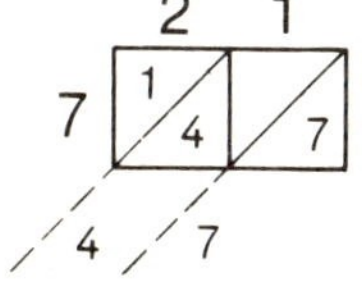

$21 \times 7 = 147$

5

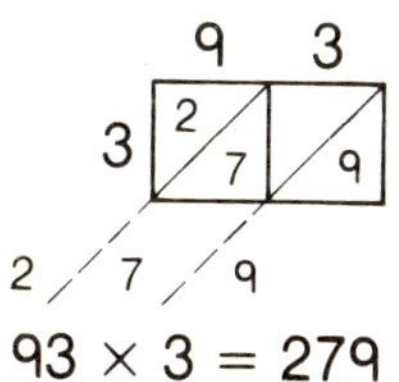

$93 \times 3 = 279$

6

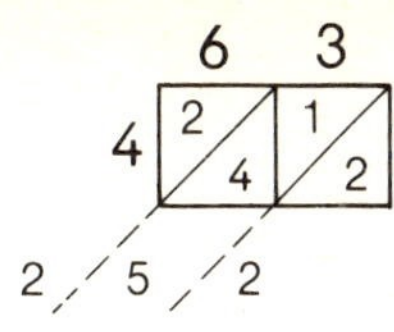

$63 \times 4 = 252$

7

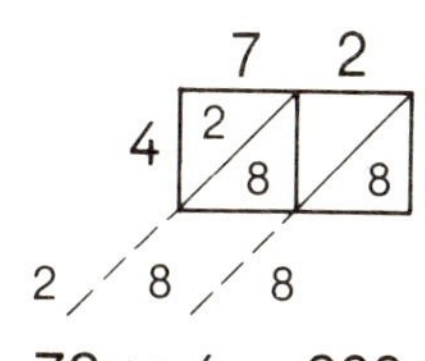

$72 \times 4 = 288$

8

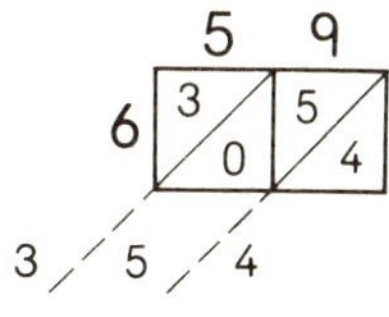

$59 \times 6 = 354$

9

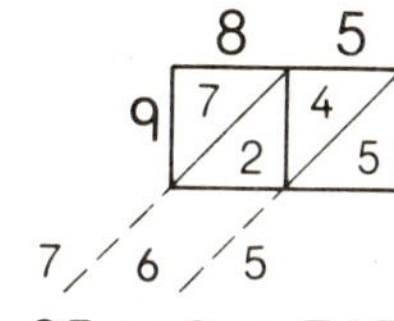

$85 \times 9 = 765$

10

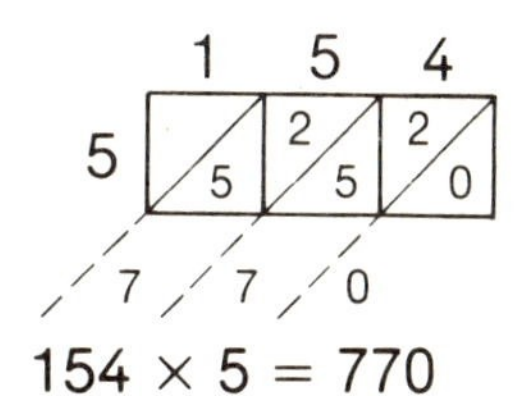

$154 \times 5 = 770$

11

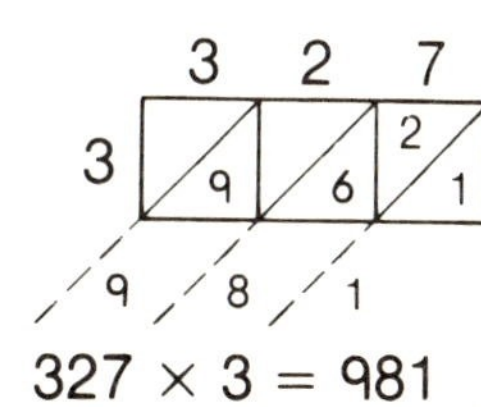

$327 \times 3 = 981$

12

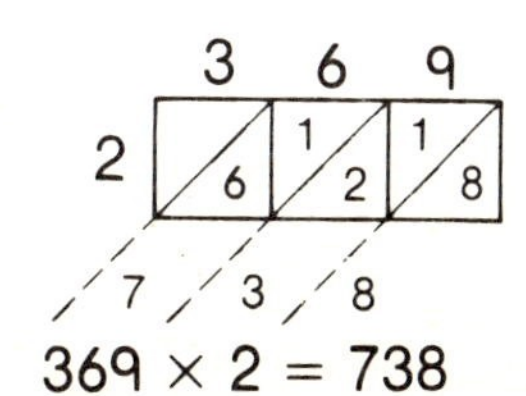

$369 \times 2 = 738$

13

	4	9	8
6	2/4	5/4	4/8

2 9 8 8

$498 \times 6 = 2988$

14

	3	8	6
7	2/1	5/6	4/2

2 7 0 2

$386 \times 7 = 2702$

15

	4	1	9
6	2/4	/6	5/4

2 5 1 4

$419 \times 6 = 2514$

C **p. 75**

1 136 × 8 and 136 × 8

1088

48 → 6 × 8
240 → 30 × 8
800 → 100 × 8
1088 → 136 × 8

2 256 × 7 and 256 × 7

1792

42 → 6 × 7
350 → 50 × 7
1400 → 200 × 7
1792 → 256 × 7

3 164 × 6 and 164 × 6

984

24 → 4 × 6
360 → 60 × 6
600 → 100 × 6
984 → 164 × 6

4 215 × 6 and 215 × 6

1290

30 → 5 × 6
60 → 10 × 6
1200 → 200 × 6
1290 → 215 × 6

5 325 × 8 and 325 × 8

2600

40 → 5 × 8
160 → 20 × 8
2400 → 300 × 8
2600 → 325 × 8

6 284 × 7 and 284 × 7

1988

28 → 4 × 7
560 → 80 × 7
1400 → 200 × 7
1988 → 284 × 7

7

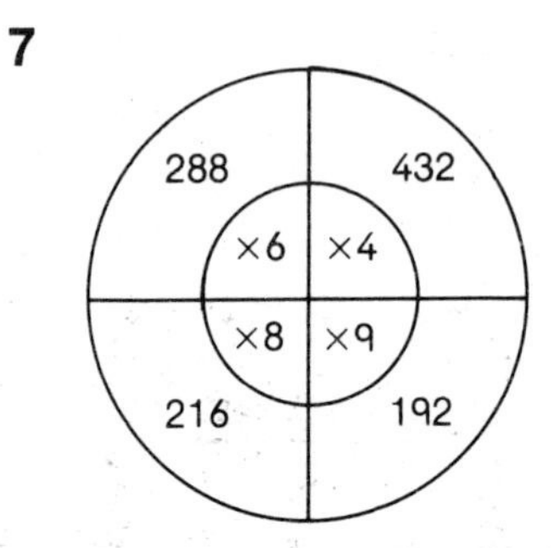

The answer is 1728.

Number 8

A **p. 76**

1 ⑩ ⑩ is $\frac{2}{10}$ of £1.

2 ⑩ ⑩ ⑩ is $\frac{3}{10}$ of £1.

3

(10) (10) (10) (10) is $\frac{4}{10}$ of £1.

(10) (10) (10) (10) (10) is $\frac{5}{10}$ of £1.

(10) (10) (10) (10) (10) (10) is $\frac{6}{10}$ of £1.

(10) (10) (10) (10) (10) (10) (10) is $\frac{7}{10}$ of £1.

(10) (10) (10) (10) (10) (10) (10) (10) is $\frac{8}{10}$ of £1.

(10) (10) (10) (10) (10) (10) (10) (10) (10) is $\frac{9}{10}$ of £1.

(10) (10) (10) (10) (10) (10) (10) (10) (10) (10) is $\frac{10}{10}$ of £1.

4 50p = £0·50
5 60p = £0·60
6 70p = £0·70
7 80p = £0·80
8 £1·20

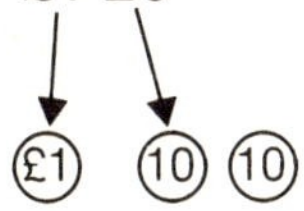

(£1) (10) (10)

9 £1·40

(£1) (10) (10) (10) (10)

10 £1·50

(£1) (10) (10) (10) (10) (10)

11 $\frac{2}{100}$ of £1 = 2p
12 $\frac{5}{100}$ of £1 = 5p
13 $\frac{7}{100}$ of £1 = 7p
14 $\frac{9}{100}$ of £1 = 9p
15 2p = £0·02
16 4p = £0·04
17 5p = £0·05
18 7p = £0·07
19 £0·09

(1)(1)(1)(1)(1)(1)(1)(1)(1)

20 £0·04

(1)(1)(1)(1)

21 £0·08

(1)(1)(1)(1)(1)(1)(1)(1)

B p. 78

1

Pence	Fraction of £1	Till shows
30p	$\frac{3}{10}$	£0·30
50p	$\frac{5}{10}$	£0·50
2p	$\frac{2}{100}$	£0·02
40p	$\frac{4}{10}$	£0·40
4p	$\frac{4}{100}$	£0·04
70p	$\frac{7}{10}$	£0·70
7p	$\frac{7}{100}$	£0·07

2 £2·98 — $\frac{9}{10}$, $\frac{8}{100}$

3 £3·79 — $\frac{7}{10}$, $\frac{9}{100}$

4 £3·67 — $\frac{6}{10}$, $\frac{7}{100}$

5 £4·17 — $\frac{1}{10}$, $\frac{7}{100}$

6 £2·75 — £2

7 £5·72
2p

8 £7·25
20p

C p. 79

1 3·52 m
3 m | 0·50 m | 0·02 m
3 m | 50 cm | 2 cm

2 5·55 m
5 m | 0·50 m | 0·05 m
5 m | 50 cm | 5 cm

3 14·21 m
14 m | 0·20 m | 0·01 m
14 m | 20 cm | 1 cm

4 7·93 m
7 m | 0·90 m | 0·03 m
7 m | 90 cm | 3 cm

5 6·08 m
6 m | 0·08 m
6 m | 8 cm

6 20·03 m
20 m | 0·03 m
20 m | 3 cm

7 10 cm is $\frac{1}{10}$ of 1 metre

8 1 cm is $\frac{1}{100}$ of 1 metre

Data 2

A p. 80

1 15
2 5 kittens
3 5
4 5
5 11
6 4
7 Largest 6
Smallest 4
Range 2
8 5
9 3
10 4
11 6
12 7
13 11
14 4
15 24
16 6
17 2
18 20 lambs
19 2
20 2

B p. 82

1 Agama Lizard
Mean 17 Range 7
2 Nile Crocodile
Mean 43 Range 18
3 Python
Mean 35 Range 42
4 Giant Tortoise
Mean 12 Range 5

5 Chameleon
Mean 29 Range 9

6 Green Turtle
Mean 104 Range 25

7 9

8 13

9 12

10 8

11 20 10

C p. 84

1 7 (to the nearest whole number)

2 8 years (to the nearest whole number)

3 Answer depends on family.

Money 2

A p. 85

1 £26

2 £42

3 £48

4 £54

5 £60

6 £83

7 £313

8

Date	Deposit	Balance
23 January	£140	£140
29 January	£100	£240
16 February	£120	£360
26 February	£130	£490
13 March	£150	£640

9 £540

B p. 87

1 Cakes £68·78

2 Snack £43·31

3 Sponge throwing £41·02

4 Lucky dip £37·23

5 Golf £46·83

6 Wellie throwing £49·74

7 £221

8 £205·85

9 £320·50

10 £421·00

11 £476·60

12 £626·85

13 £315·27

14 £420·00

C p. 89

1 £604·02

2 £504·02

3 £566·40

4 £450·53

Shape 2

A p. 90

2 scalene triangle

3 isosceles triangle

4 equilateral triangle

5 isosceles triangle

6 isosceles triangle pennant

7 The yellow geostrips are parallel.

8 The blue geostrips are parallel.

9 geostrip ladder

10 Various colours are possible but the pairs of parallel lines are shown here.

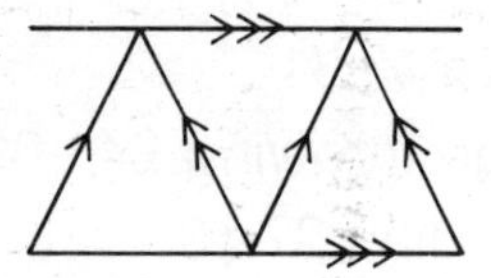

11 The yellow straws are parallel and vertical.

12 The green straws are parallel and horizontal.

13 straw pattern

14 horizontal and vertical chart

15 horizontal and vertical lists

17 The opposite sides of the shapes must be parallel.

18 The opposite sides are still parallel and are all the same length.

19 

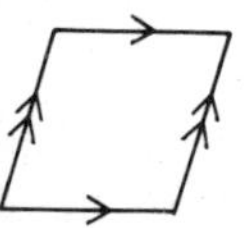

20 The opposite sides are still parallel and equal in length.

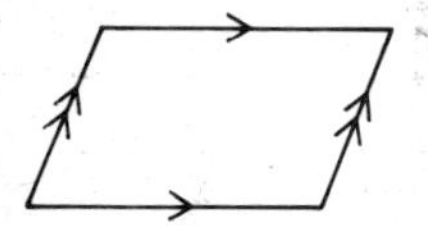

B p. 94

1 is box B.

2 is box D.

3 is box C.

4 is box A.

5
6 } geostrip quadrilaterals

7 The quadrilaterals are rigid.

8 The new shapes are triangles. Various drawings are possible.

9 the triangle

10
11
12

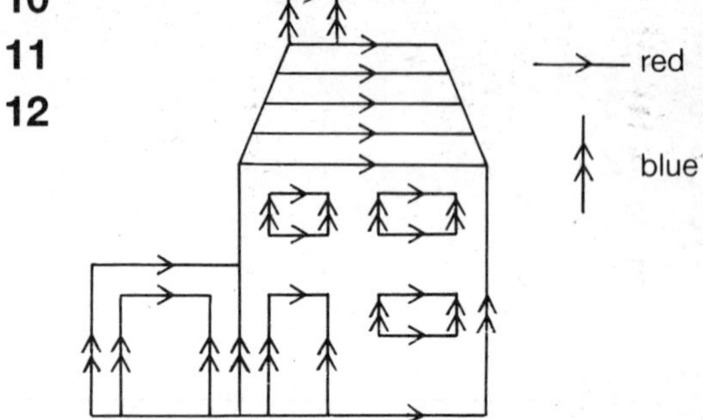

13 The green lines are not horizontal, vertical or parallel.

14 parallel lines

15 non-parallel lines

16 Parallel lines are the same distance apart and can be different lengths. They never meet or cross.

C p. 96

1 The triangle is rigid.

2 The shapes need these extra geostrips to make them rigid.
triangle 0 square 1 pentagon 2
hexagon 3

3 various answers.

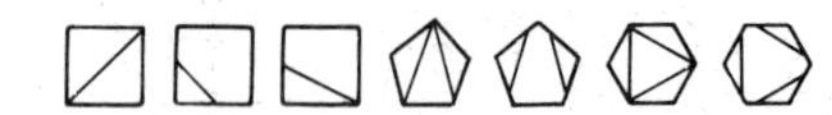

4 Triangles are used because a triangle is a rigid shape.

Book 2

Number 9

A p. 4

1	5
2	15
3	10
4	4
5	8
6	16
7	12
8	10
9	20

B p. 5

1	4
2	12
3	28
4	36
5	$\frac{2}{10}$
6	8
7	32
8	16
9	40
10	24
11	6
12	18
13	42
14	30
15	$\frac{2}{8}$

Time 2

A p. 8

1

10 a.m.	10:00
11 a.m.	11:00
noon	12:00
1 p.m.	13:00
2 p.m.	14:00

2

10 p.m.	22:00
11 p.m.	23:00
midnight	00:00
1 a.m.	01:00
2 a.m.	02:00

3

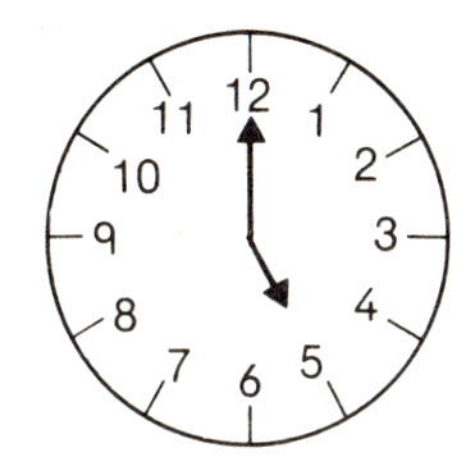

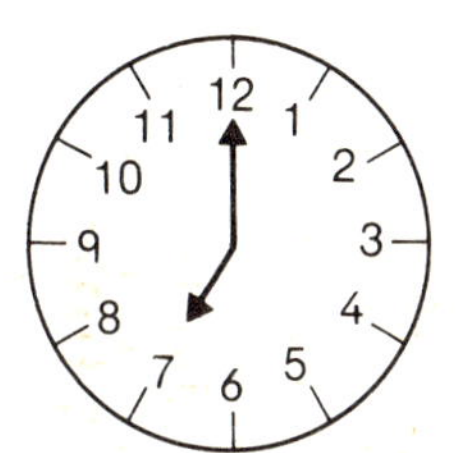

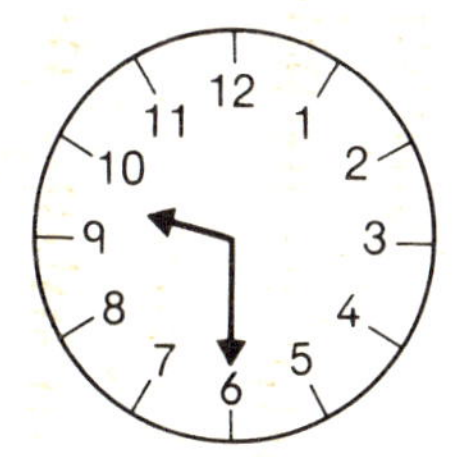

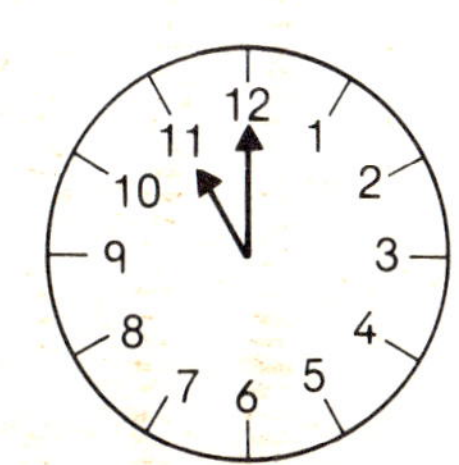

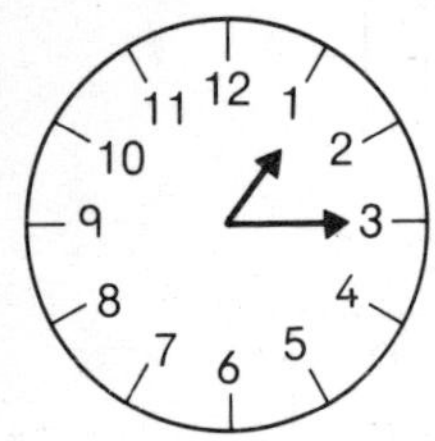

4 $2\frac{1}{2}$ hrs or 2 hrs 30 mins.

5 2 hrs

6 8 hrs

7

10:15 a.m.
2:30 p.m.
5:00 p.m.
8:15 p.m.

8

08:00
12:00
15:00
17:15

9

07:45
11:30
14:15
16:45

B p. 10

1

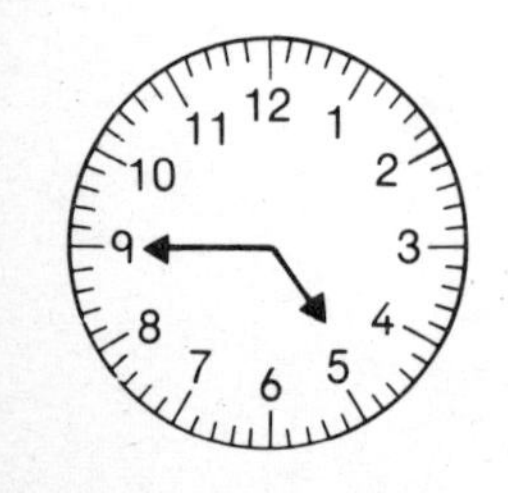

2

3

4

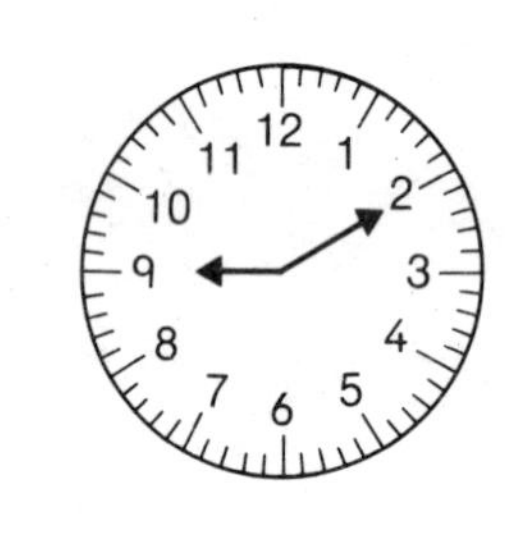

5

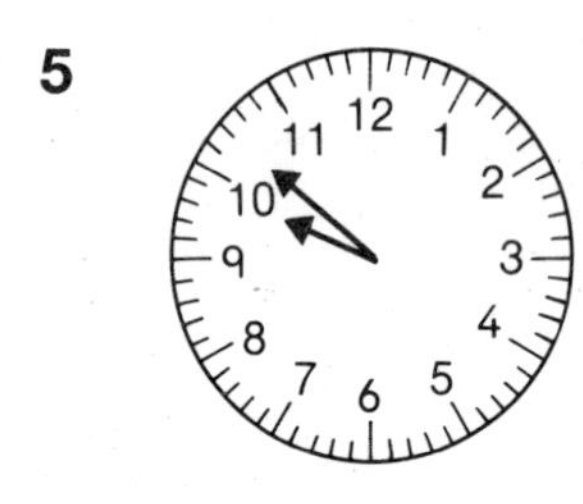

6

7

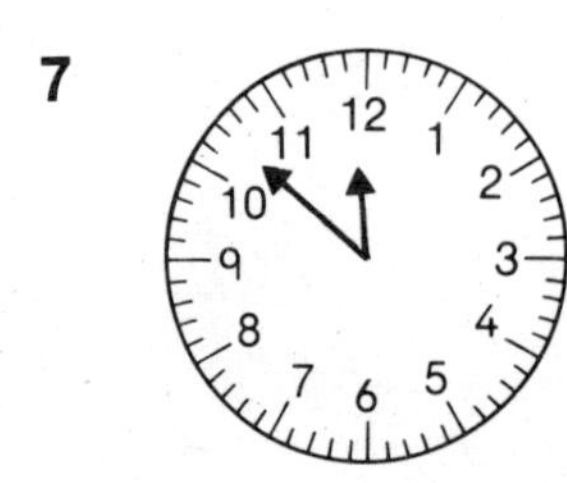

8

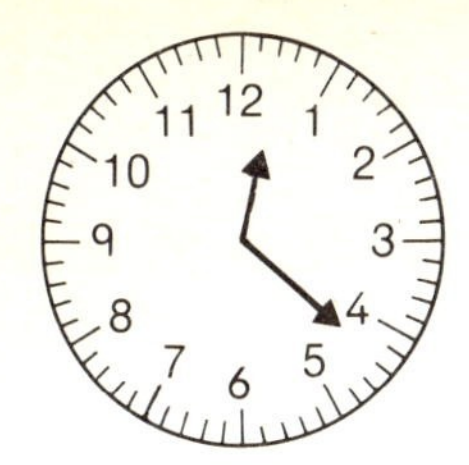

9

10

11 4 hrs 10 mins

12 42 mins

13 1 hr 1 min

14 59 mins

15 30 mins

16 4 hrs 17 mins

17 15 hrs

C **p. 12**

1 120 hrs 30 min

2 47 hrs 30 mins

3 The sum of **1** and **2** should equal 168 hours (total hours in 1 week).

4 12:52 → 12:56 → 13:00 → 13:04 → 13:08 → 13:12 → 13:16 → 13:20 → 13:24 → 13:28

5 23:54 → 23:58 → 00:02 → 00:06 → 00:10 →00:14 → 00:18 → 00:22 → 00:26

6 11 trains

20:37 20:41 20:45 20:49
20:53 20:57 21:01 21:05
21:09 21:13 21:17

Co-ordinates

A **p. 13**

1–10

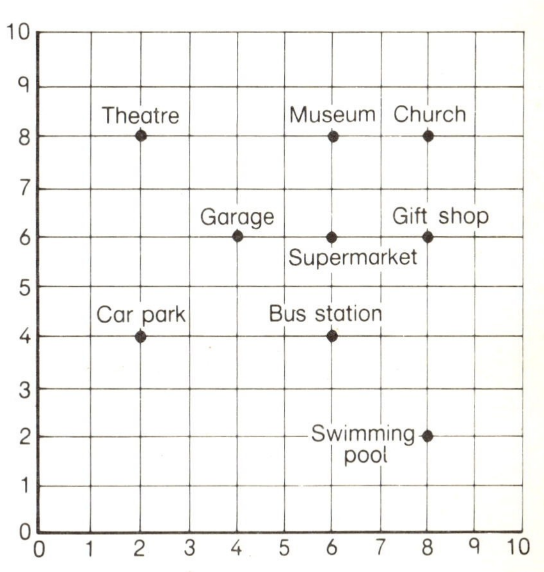

11 Garage or Museum

12 Possible answers include
Church – E
Gift Shop – SE
Supermarket or Bus Station – S
Garage or Car Park – SW
Theatre – W

13 Possible answers include:
Museum or Supermarket – N
Gift shop – NE

Swimming Pool – SE
Car Park – W
Theatre or Garage – NW

14 (5, 12)
15 (9, 12)
16 (11, 18)
17 (7, 18)
18 (7, 6)
19 (9, 20)
20 (11, 4)

B p. 15

Other answers may be possible.

1 Cliff Top Cafe (11, 16)
2 Airport (7, 6)
3 Beach Stores (3, 10)
Watersports Centre (3, 18)
4 Windsurfing Centre (3, 4)
5 Craft Centre (9, 6)
Pottery (9, 12)
Wood Carving (7, 14)
6 Bird Reserve (7, 10)
7 Watersports Centre (3, 18)
8 Castle (3, 16)
Motor Museum (3, 14)
9 Gull Rock Island (9, 20)
Lighthouse (11, 18)
10 Sports Centre (11, 10)
Watersports Centre (3, 18)
11 Motor Museum (3, 14)
12 Rare Animals Farm (3, 6)
Bird Reserve (7, 10)
Butterfly Farm (5, 12)
13 These answers depend on which places are chosen for the tour.
14 Corfu
15 Cyprus

16 Iceland
17 Sicily
18 Finding islands using a map of the world.
19 Mull (5, 5) (1, 5) (4, 3) (4, 3)
20 Skye (4, 1) (3, 5) (5, 4) (1, 1)
21 Arran (1, 3) (3, 3) (3, 3) (1, 3) (2, 1)
22 Iona (5, 2) (3, 4) (2, 1) (1, 3)
23 Finding islands using a map of Britain.

C p. 17

1

A hexagon

2 (1, 1) → (3, 1) → (5, 3) → (5, 5) → (3, 5) → (1, 3) → (1, 1)

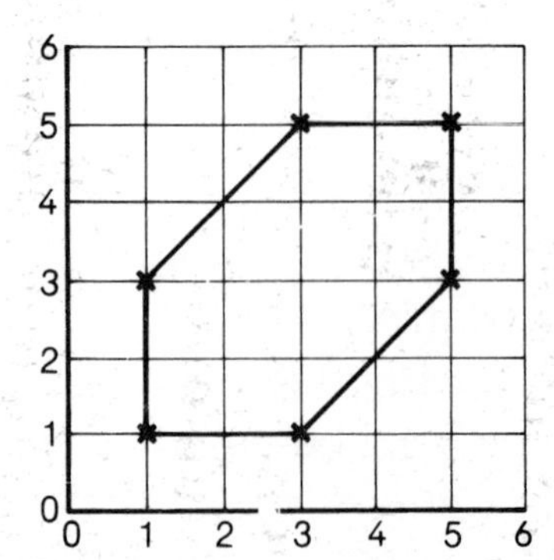

You have made the same shape.

3

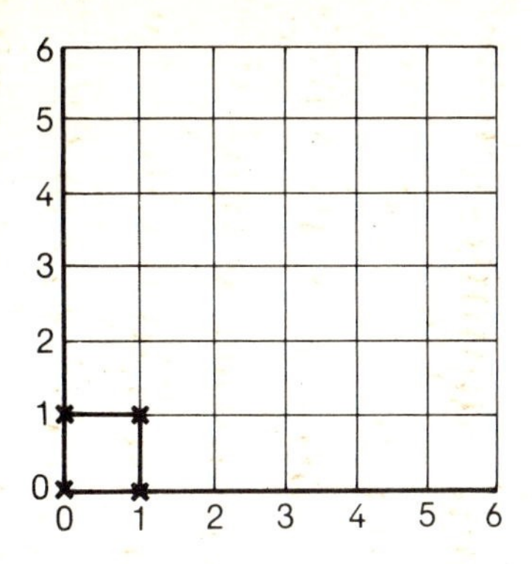

A square.

4 (0, 0) → (1, 0) → (1, 1) → (0, 1) → (0, 0)

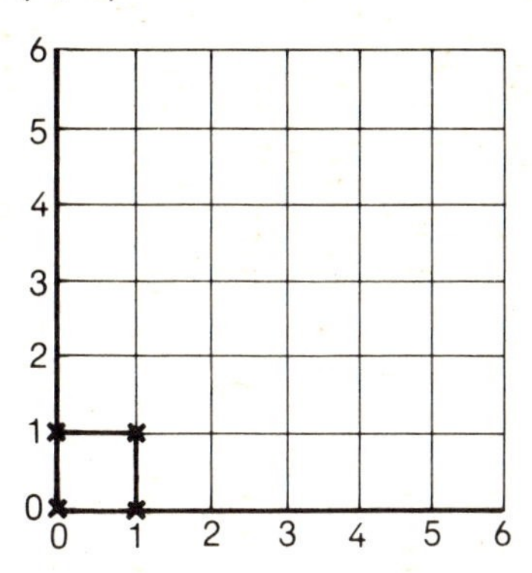

A square.

Number 10

A p. 18

1 Friday

2 Various explanations are possible.

3

Monday	3637 →	4000
Tuesday	2086 →	2000
Wednesday	1972 →	2000
Thursday	2714 →	3000
Friday	4393 →	4000

4 and **5**

4		5
Mon. / Tue.	5723	6000
Tue. / Wed.	4058	4000
Wed. / Thur.	4686	5000
Thur. / Fri.	7107	7000

6 Tuesday and Wednesday (4000)

7

Cars	2451
Vans and lorries	1529
Coaches	283
Motor bikes	130

B p. 20

1 5088

2 6294

3 5176

4 5088

5 Jan. Feb. Mar. / Oct. Nov. Dec.

6 April May June

7 May: Two thousand two hundred and sixty five.

8 June: Two thousand and thirty four.

9 July: One thousand eight hundred and ten.

10 August: One thousand six hundred and fourteen.

11 2265 + 2034 = 4299

12 1574 + 1604 = 3178

13 1614 + 1752 = 3366

14 1752 + 1952 = 3704

15 1667 + 1469 = 3136

16 1604 + 1910 = 3514

17 1995 + 2265 = 4260

18 1952 + 1667 = 3619

19

20

Jan	1600
Feb	1600
Mar	1900
April	2000
May	2300
June	2000
July	1800
Aug	1600
Sept	1800
Oct	2000
Nov	1700
Dec	1500

21 December is the odd one out because it rounds to 1000. All the rest round to 2000.

22 $1910 < 1995$

23 $1574 > 1469$

24 $1604 < 1614$

25 4800

C p. 22

1 6730 + 5321

2 5321 + 7810 or 5609 + 7395

3 6730 + 7395

4 7810 + 7395

Data 3

A p. 23

1 3°C

2 6°C

3 8°C

4 10 a.m.

5 10:30 a.m. or 3:00 p.m.

6 11:30 a.m. or 2:00 p.m.

7 1 hour

8 3°C

9 4°C

10 5°C

11 6 hours

12

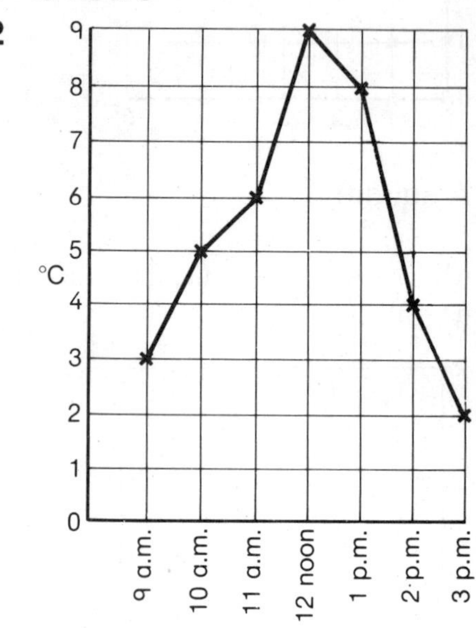

B p. 24

1 −1°C

2 5°C

3 5°C

4 −3°C

5 11 hours

6 13 hours

7 11 a.m. 3 p.m.

8 1°C

9 4°C

10 −2°C

11 Probably winter. The temperature drops below zero.

12 13 14

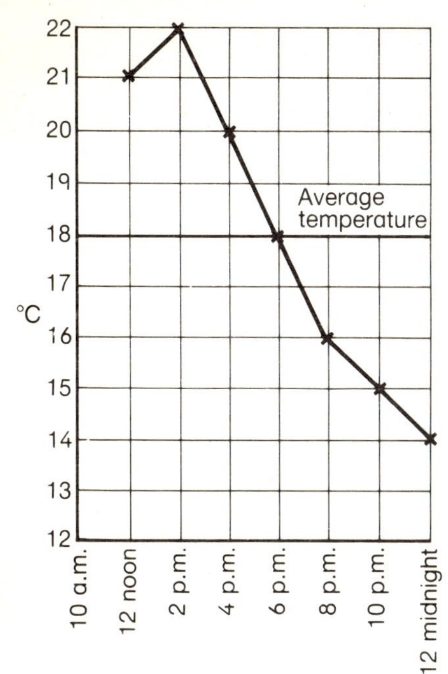

15 Various sentences are possible.

C p. 25

1 Wednesday was 20°C
Monday was 18°C
Thursday was 17°C
Tuesday was 15°C
Friday was 14°C

2

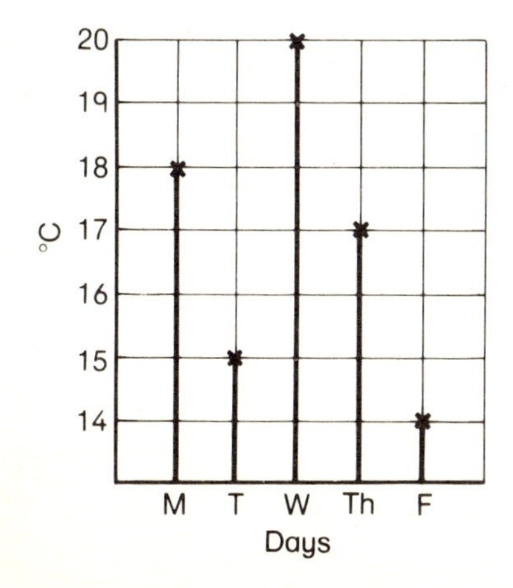

Number 11

A p. 26

1 I II III IV V VI VII VIII IX X

2	22	**3**	26
4	35	**5**	38
6	43	**7**	59
8	64	**9**	96
10	XXV	**11**	XXIX
12	XXXVII	**13**	XLI
14	LXVIII	**15**	LXXXII
16	LXXIII	**17**	XCIV

18 DCC
19 DCCC
20 112
21 225
22 130
23 350
24 510
25 421
26 254
27 310
28 620
29 1200
30 1300
31 1330
32 1113
33 1500
34 CM
35 0 (zero)
36 2064
37 2289
38 3521
39 4396
40 1918

41 2794
42 1900
43 3929

B p. 29

1 1970 2 1980
3 1960 4 1975
5 MCMLXXX
6 MCMI
7 MCMLVI
8 MCMLXIII
9 MCMXCI
10 MCMXXIV
11 MM
12 Answer depends on the current year.
13 28 years
14 35 years
15 17 years

C p. 30

1–6 Answers depend on the shape chosen to show 100 and the method used to position the numbers.

Angles 1

A p. 31

1 90°
2 180°
3 90°
4 60°
5 60°
6 90°
7 120°
8 270°
9 20°
10 40°
11 50°
12 30°
13 40°
14 90°
15 20°
16 50°
17 60°
18 60°
19 80°

B p. 34

1 very cold 10°
cold 40°
warm 70°
hot 30°
very hot 30°

2–5 Estimates of wind dial angles.
6 light wind 60° no wind 50°
strong wind 30° gale 40°
7 A straight angle.

C p. 35

1 250°
2 90°
3 130°
4 310°
5 60°

Shape 3

A p. 36

1 A B D G H

2 H 3 G

4 A 5 B

6 D

7 Prism made from net.

8 Rectangular prism or cuboid

9 A rectangle.

10 Gift box made from net.

11 Square based pyramid

12 Square

13

14 The base is a triangle.

B p. 38

1 2 faces are squares
4 faces are rectangles

2 8 faces are rectangles
2 faces are octagons

3 3 faces are rectangles
2 faces are triangles

4 6 faces are rectangles
2 faces are hexagons

5 6 faces are rectangles

6

Shape	Faces	Vertices	Edges
Rectangular prism	6	8	12
Square based pyramid	5	5	8
Triangular based pyramid	4	4	6
Cube	6	8	12

7 Faces + Vertices = Edges + 2
Other answers are possible.

C p. 40

Other nets are possible and flaps may be added.

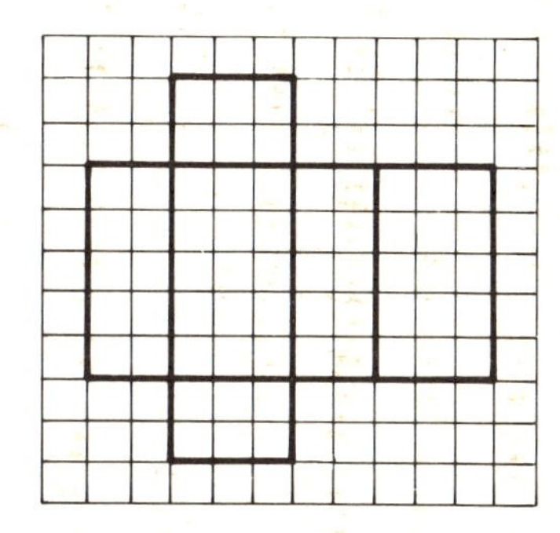

2

3

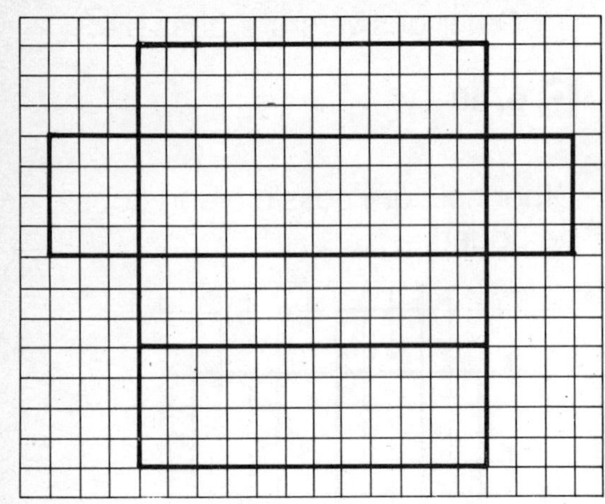

Number 12

A p. 41

1 56 days
2 8 weeks
3 14 weeks
4 Quicker. It took 6 weeks to return.
5 38 km
6 16 km
7 23 km
8 27 km
9 28 km
10 34 km

B p. 42

1 65 days (Counting 1st. Nov.)
2 9 weeks 2 days
3 115 days
4 184 days
5 230 days
6 11 weeks 2 days
7 5 weeks
8 10 weeks 1 day

C p. 43

1 75 km 2 89 km
3 113 km 4 67 km
5 68 km 6 89 km

Data 4

A p. 44

1

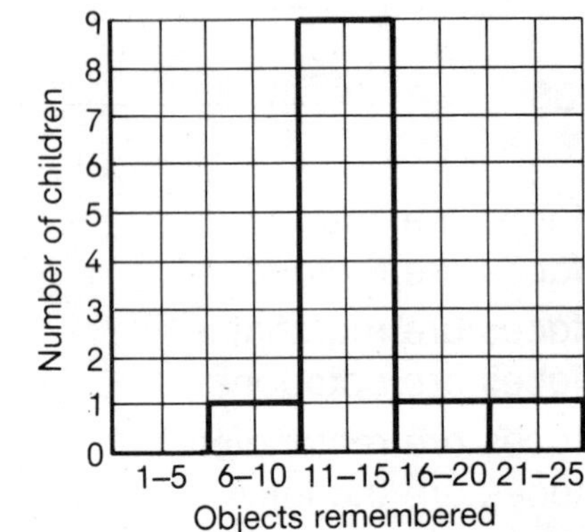

2 Yes (probably). There are fewer scores below 11.
3 The children have had practice. Other explanations are possible.
4 1–4 5–8 9–12 13–16 17–20
5

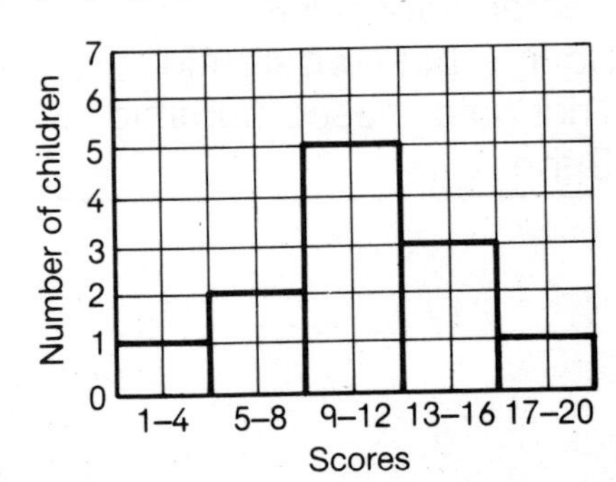

B p. 46

1

Score group	1–10	11–20	21–30	31–40	41–50	51–60	61–70
Number of children	4	2	4	3	4	1	2

2

Number of children

0 1 2 3 4 5 6 7

1–10 11–20 21–30 31–40 41–50 51–60 61–70

Score group

3 Graph showing scores for skipping. Answers depend on how many children are chosen for each group.

C p. 48

Tables showing the scores that each child might have got.

Area

A p. 49

1 Area = 15 cm^2

2 Area = 16 cm^2

3 Area = 24 cm^2

4 Area = 30 cm^2

5

	Length	Width	Area
Fizzo	5 cm	3 cm	15 cm^2
Soda	4 cm	4 cm	16 cm^2
Quench	4 cm	6 cm	24 cm^2
Pop	6 cm	5 cm	30 cm^2

6 Pop

7 Fizzo

8 Area = 18 cm^2

9 Area = 20 cm^2

10 Area = 10 cm^2

11 Area = 32 cm^2

12

	Length	Width	Area
Suds	6 cm	3 cm	18 cm^2
Washo	5 cm	4 cm	20 cm^2
Clean	2 cm	5 cm	10 cm^2
Bright	8 cm	4 cm	32 cm^2

B p. 51

	Length	Width	Area	Perimeter
1	5 cm	7 cm	35 cm^2	24 cm
2	5 cm	3 cm	15 cm^2	16 cm
3	5 cm	8 cm	40 cm^2	26 cm
4	5 cm	4 cm	20 cm^2	18 cm
5	10 cm	5 cm	50 cm^2	30 cm
6	5 cm	4 cm	20 cm^2	18 cm
7	5 cm	5 cm	25 cm^2	20 cm
8	10 cm	2 cm	20 cm^2	24 cm
9	10 cm	3 cm	30 cm^2	26 cm

10 64 cm

11 Area = 1 cm^2 Perimeter = 4 cm

12 Area = 4 cm^2 Perimeter = 8 cm

13 Area = 9 cm^2
Perimeter = 12 cm

14 Area = 16 cm^2
Perimeter = 16 cm

15

Length	Width	Area	Perimeter
1 cm	1 cm	1 cm^2	4 cm
2 cm	2 cm	4 cm^2	8 cm
3 cm	3 cm	9 cm^2	12 cm
4 cm	4 cm	16 cm^2	16 cm
5 cm	5 cm	25 cm^2	20 cm
6 cm	6 cm	36 cm^2	24 cm

16 49 cm^2

17 32 cm

18 Photographs cut to an area of 48 cm^2.

19 Two rectangles. Each one 8 cm by 12 cm.

20

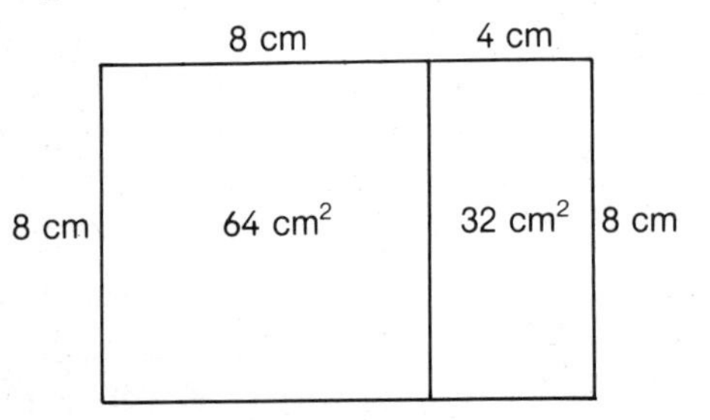

21

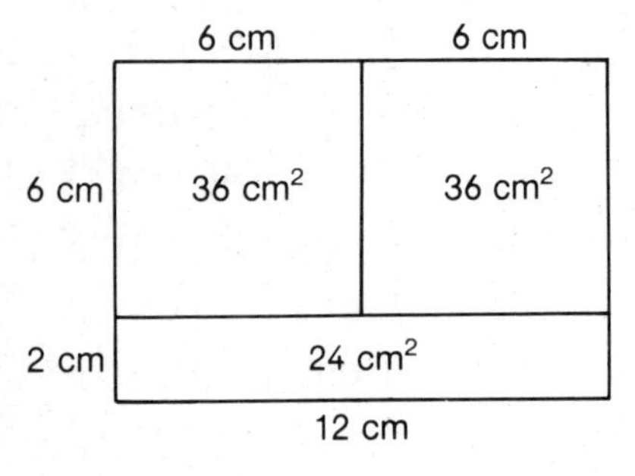

C p. 53

1 Answers depend on the advertisements chosen.

Data 5

A p. 54

1 50 miles
2 75 miles
3 2 hours
4 125 miles
5 150 miles
6 150 miles
7 200 miles
8 1 hour
9 50 miles
10

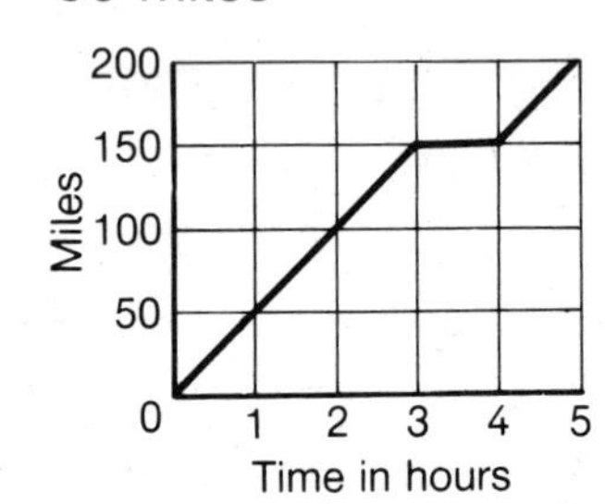

B p. 56

1

Units on phonecard	0	1	2	3	4	5	6	7	8	9	10
Cost in pence	0	10	20	30	40	50	60	70	80	90	100

2 7

3 90p

4

Cost in pence
100
90
80
70
60
50
40
30
20
10
0
1 2 3 4 5 6 7 8 9 10
Units on phonecard

5 100 miles

6 100 miles

7 50 miles

8 10 miles

9

Time	1 p.m.	2 p.m.	3 p.m.
Miles	0	50	100

Time	4 p.m.	5 p.m.	6 p.m.
Miles	100	150	160

C p. 58

1

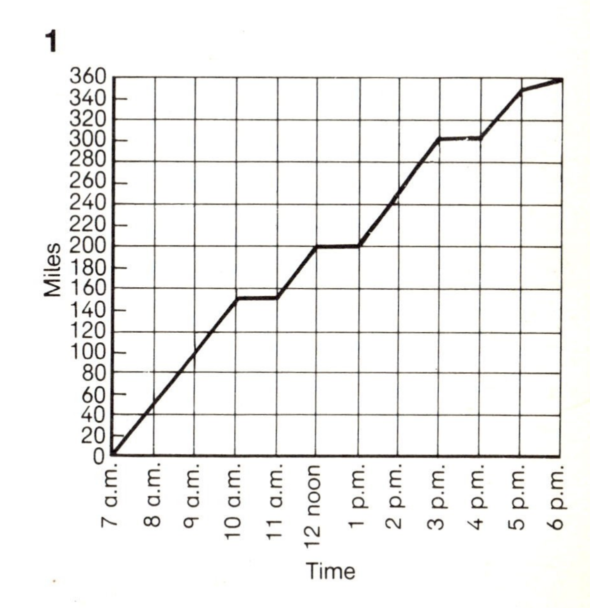

2 360 miles

3 11 hours

4 Before lunch.

Weight 2

A p. 59

	Allosaurus	2000 kg	2·000 tonnes
1	Iguanodon	4500 kg	4·500 tonnes
2	Stegosaurus	1800 kg	1·800 tonnes
3	Torvosaurus	5400 kg	5·400 tonnes

4 Iguanodon
5 Torvosaurus
6 Torvosaurus
7 Allosaurus
8 Torvosaurus
9 Iguanodon
10 1000 kg or 1·000 tonnes
11 200 kg or 0·200 tonnes
12 3400 kg or 3·400 tonnes
13 Allosaurus 2 tonnes
Tyrannosaurus 6 tonnes
Stegosaurus 2 tonnes
Torvosaurus 5 tonnes
14 6
15 2
16 5

B **p. 61**

1

Megalosaurus	900 kg
Iguanodon	4500 kg
Triceratops	5400 kg
Tyrannosaurus	6400 kg

2 1900 kg
3 3600 kg
4 5500 kg
5 900 kg
6 6 times heavier. Various explanations are possible.
7 5
8 Megalosaurus and Iguanodon balance Triceratops.
9

Diplodocus	11 tonnes
Triceratops	5 tonnes
Tyrannosaurus	6 tonnes
Megalosaurus	1 tonne

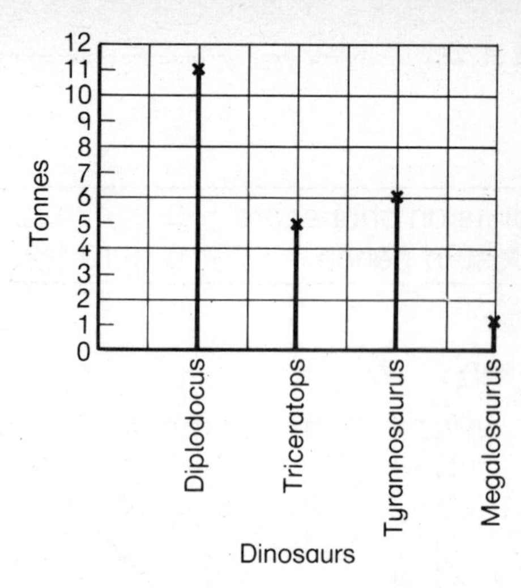

Other graphs are possible

10 100 **11** 9
12 16 or 17 **13** 20

C p. 63

		Basic weight	Fattest weight
1	Ultrasaurus	about 48 tonnes	about 64 tonnes
2	Brachiosaurus	about 36 tonnes	about 48 tonnes
3	Titanosaurus	about 54 tonnes	about 72 tonnes

4

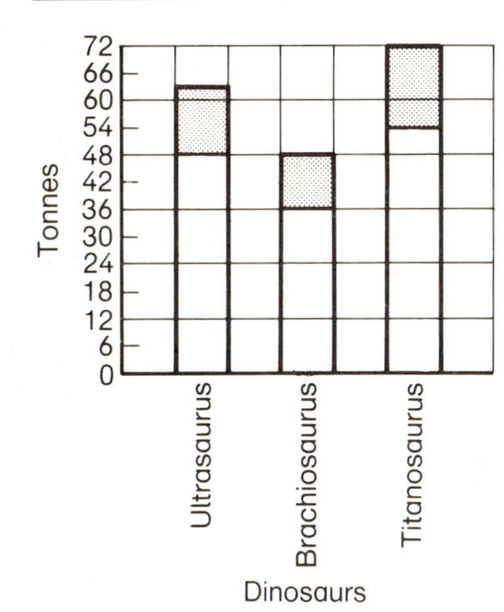

14 £400
15 £426
16 £26

B p. 66

	Cost per person	Cost per child	Total
1	£192	£185	£377
2	£278	£273	£551
3	£236	£218	£454
4	£133	£125	£258
5	£454		
6	£312		
7	£606		
8	£418		
9	£267		
10	£209		
11	£324		
12	£753		
13	£178		

C p. 68

1 £2145
2 £2940
3 7 December to 31 December
4 1 June to 30 June

Money 3

A p. 64

1

Date	Cost	Hotel
24 March	£80	Fisherman
5 April	£87	Majestic
28 March	£82	Royal
1 April	£90	Anchor

2 £156 3 £168
4 £160 5 £180
6 £281
7 £151
8 £358
9 £200

10 By air.
11 By air.
12 By rail.
13 By air.

Probability 2

A p. 69

1 3 ways.

2

1st dice	2nd dice	Total
2	3	5
3	2	5
1	4	5
4	1	5

3

1st dice	2nd dice	Total
6	1	7
1	6	7
5	2	7
2	5	7
4	3	7
3	4	7

4

1st dice	2nd dice	Total
4	6	10
5	5	10
6	4	10

5 3 ways

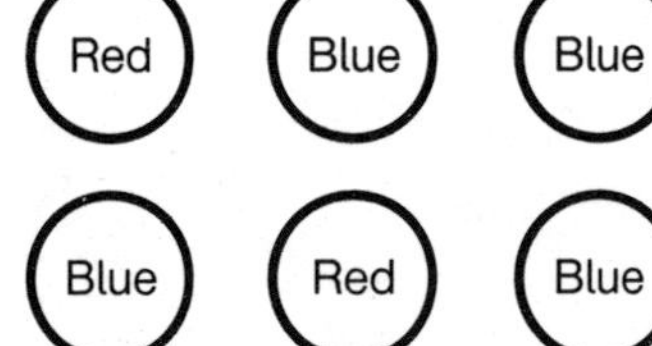

6 6 ways

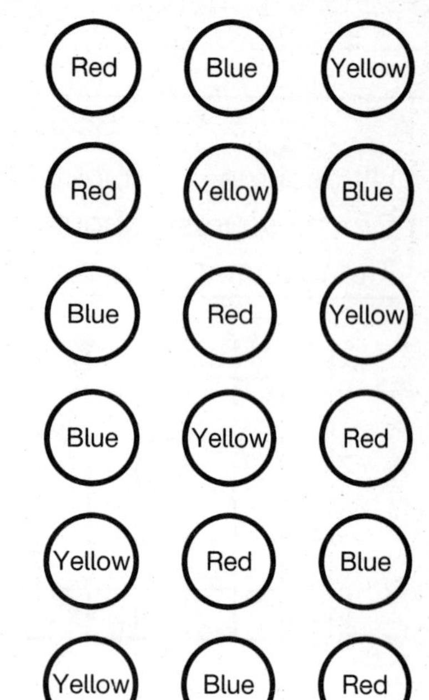

7 Yes.

B p. 71

1

2

Colour of shorts	Colour of top
Blue	Red
Blue	Blue
Blue	Green
Blue	Orange
White	Red
White	Blue
White	Green
White	Orange
Yellow	Red
Yellow	Blue
Yellow	Green
Yellow	Orange

3 12 kits

4 8 kits

5 4 kits

6 16 kits

7 A — B
A — C
A — D
B — C
B — D
C — D

8 A — B
A — C
A — D
A — E
B — C
B — D
B — E
C — D
C — E
D — E

C **p. 73**

1

Game 1 Win or Lose

Game 2 W or L W or L

Game 3 W or L W or L W or L W or L

2 First way W → W → L
Second way W → L → W
Third way L → W → W

Shape 4

A **p. 74**

1 A template made from a square.

2

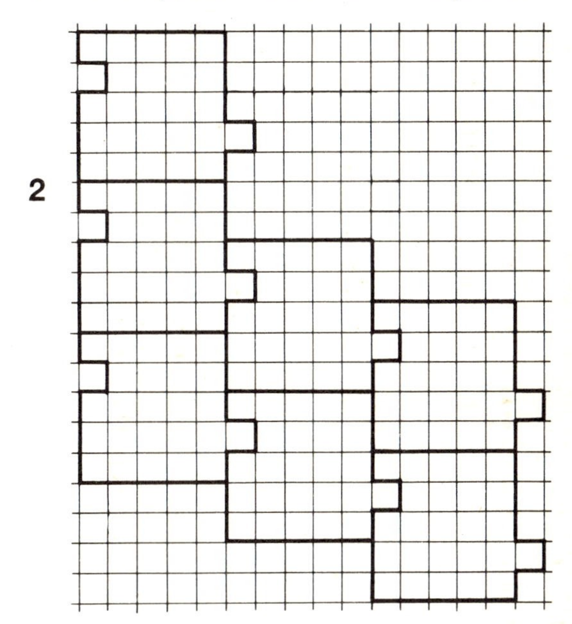

3

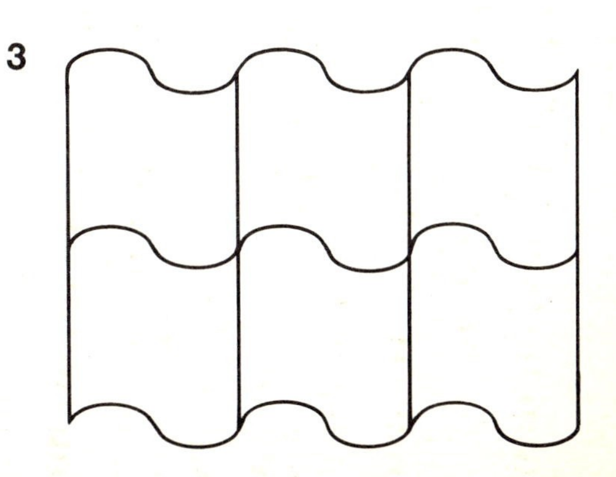

B p. 76

1

2 Rectangular template and tessellating pattern.

C p. 78

Square templates and design.

Number 13

A p. 79

1 $\frac{1}{4} + \frac{2}{4} = \frac{3}{4}$ $\frac{1}{4}$ not finished
2 $\frac{3}{8} + \frac{2}{8} = \frac{5}{8}$ $\frac{3}{8}$ not finished
3 $\frac{1}{5} + \frac{2}{5} = \frac{3}{5}$ $\frac{2}{5}$ not finished
4 $\frac{2}{6} + \frac{1}{6} = \frac{3}{6}$ $\frac{3}{6}$ not finished
5 $\frac{1}{6} + \frac{4}{6} = \frac{5}{6}$
6 $\frac{2}{5} + \frac{1}{5} = \frac{3}{5}$
7 $\frac{1}{4} + \frac{1}{4} + \frac{1}{4} + \frac{1}{4} = \frac{4}{4} = 1$ whole shape
8 $\frac{1}{3} + \frac{1}{3} + \frac{1}{3} = \frac{3}{3} = 1$ whole shape
9 $1 + \frac{1}{2} = 1\frac{1}{2}$

B p. 81

1 $\frac{3}{5} + \frac{1}{5} = \frac{4}{5}$
2 $\frac{2}{6} + \frac{2}{6} = \frac{4}{6}$
3 $\frac{4}{8} + \frac{3}{8} = \frac{7}{8}$
4 $\frac{2}{12} + \frac{7}{12} = \frac{9}{12}$
5 $\frac{3}{10} + \frac{4}{10} = \frac{7}{10}$
6 $\frac{3}{12} + \frac{6}{12} = \frac{9}{12}$
7 $\frac{2}{10} + \frac{3}{10} + \frac{4}{10} = \frac{9}{10}$
8 $\frac{3}{8} + \frac{1}{8} + \frac{2}{8} = \frac{6}{8}$
9 $\frac{4}{12} + \frac{2}{12} + \frac{3}{12} = \frac{9}{12}$
10 $\frac{5}{12} + \frac{2}{12} + \frac{4}{12} = \frac{11}{12}$
11 $1 + 1 + \frac{3}{4} = 2\frac{3}{4}$
12 $1 + \frac{4}{6} = 1\frac{4}{6}$
13 $1 + 1 + \frac{2}{5} + \frac{1}{5} = 2\frac{3}{5}$

C p. 82

1

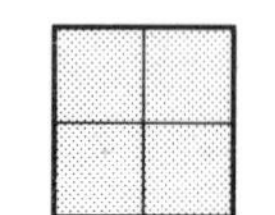

$\frac{6}{4} = \frac{4}{4} + \frac{2}{4} = 1\frac{2}{4}$

2

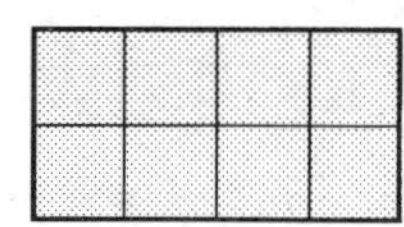

$\frac{9}{8} = \frac{8}{8} + \frac{1}{8} = 1\frac{1}{8}$

3

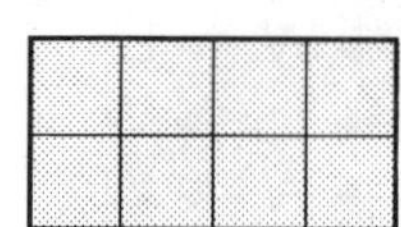

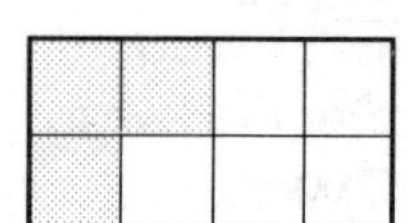

$\frac{11}{8} = \frac{8}{8} + \frac{3}{8} = 1\frac{3}{8}$

4

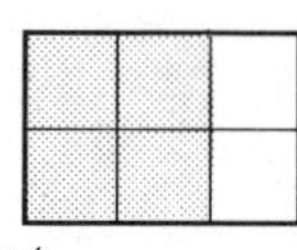

$\frac{10}{6} = \frac{6}{6} + \frac{4}{6} = 1\frac{4}{6}$

Angles 2

A p. 83

1

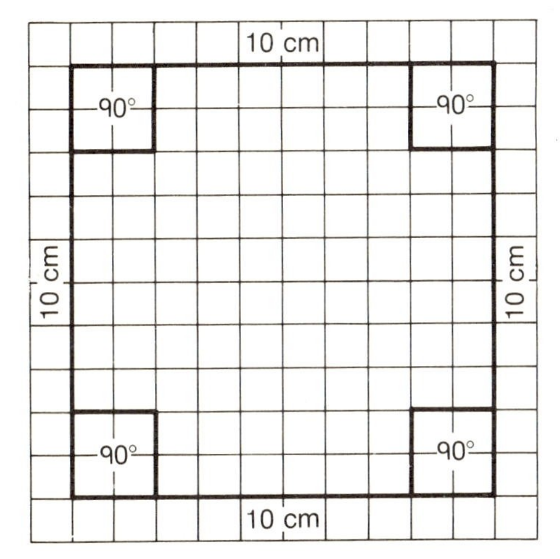

2 $90° + 90° + 90° + 90° = 360°$

3 All the angles add up to 360°.

4 360°

5

10 cm
90°
90°
7 cm
7 cm
90°
90°
10 cm

6 4

7 Two triangles.

8 $55° + 90° + 35° = 180°$

9 $55° + 90° + 35° = 180°$

10 180°

B p. 85

1 55°

2 120°

3 40°

4 95°

5 25°

6 $a = 45°$ $b = 45°$

7 $a = 70°$ $b = 85°$

8

9 $60° + 80° + 40° = 180°$

10 $55° + 65° + 60° = 180°$

11 180°

12 180°

C p. 87

1 90° 2 115°

3 70° 4 45°

5

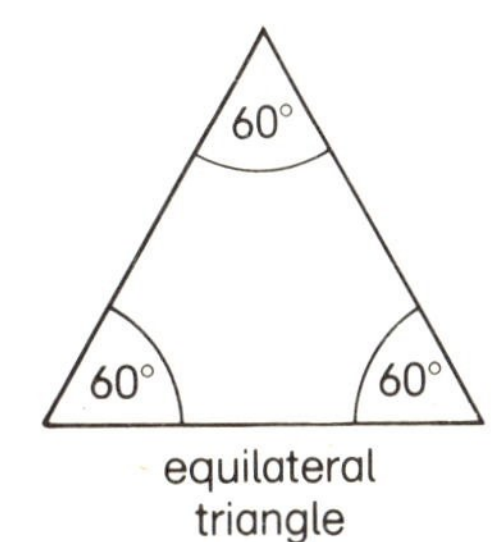

equilateral triangle

6

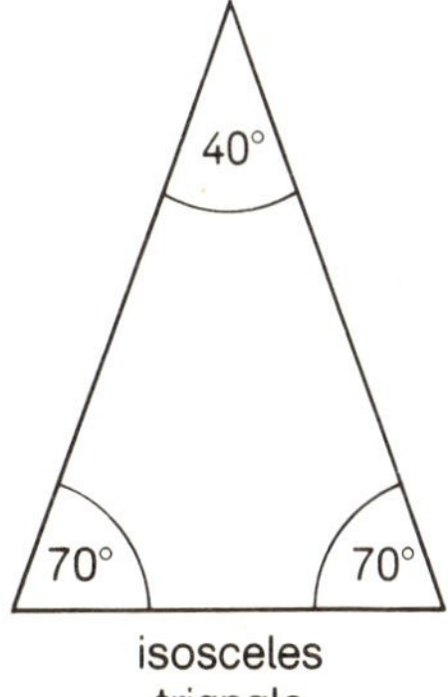

isosceles triangle

7

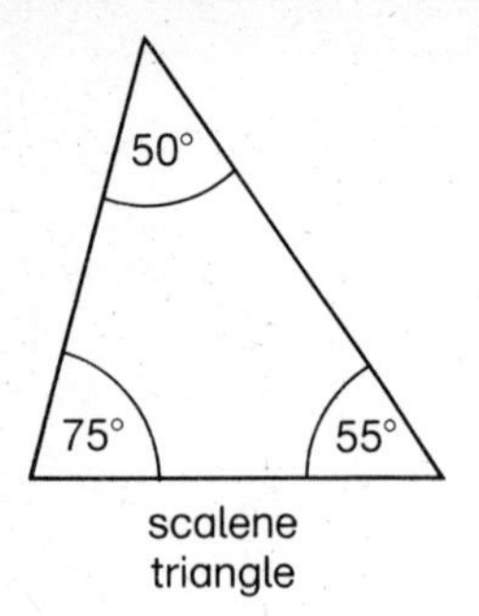

scalene triangle

Time 3

A p. 88

1

Depart Manchester	Arrive London
06:45	07:40
07:45	08:40
08:45	09:40
09:45	10:40
10:45	11:40
11:45	12:40
12:45	13:40
13:45	14:40
14:45	15:40
15:45	16:40
16:45	17:40
17:45	18:40
18:45	19:40
19:45	20:40

2 Hourly. 14 flights a day.
3 06:45
4 19:45
5 16:40
6 11:45

7

Depart Manchester	Arrive London	Allow 2 hours	Next Flight	
10:45	11:40	13:40	Singapore	14:00
07:45	08:40	10:40	St. Louis	11:00
09:45	10:40	12:40	Nice	12:40
15:45	16:40	18:40	Tokyo	19:00
16:45	17:40	19:40	Sydney	19:45

8 2 hours 5 minutes

B p. 90

1 1011
2 1255
3 1302
4 1429
5 0920 1020 1140
6 1152

C p. 91

	Travel from	Arrive at Paddington	Time to get to Euston	Leave Euston	Arrive at
	Weston-super-Mare	12:04	Allow 1 hour	13:30	Stafford at 15:15
1	Weston-super-Mare	13:18	Allow 1 hour	14:30	Milton Keynes at 15:07
2	Weston-super-Mare	15:22	Allow 1 hour	17:05	Holyhead at 21:43
3	Weston-super-Mare	14:22	Allow 1 hour	16:00	Crewe at 17:54

Length 2

A p. 92

1 1141 m
2 3200 m
3 1344 m
4 1024 m
5 1424 m
6 812 m
7 gardens
8 squirrels
9 2·377 km **10** 1·953 km
11 2·579 km
12 goats → gardens 2·215 km
goats → birds → gardens
2·448 km
0·233 km difference
13 160 m
14 0·160 km
15 40 m

B p. 94

1 1·056 km **2** 1·230 km
3 1·822 km **4** 1·021 km
5 1·143 km **6** 1·711 km
7 2·286 km **8** 2·843 km
9 2·853 km **10** 3·399 km
11 3·997 km
12 3·494 km
13 36 m
14 56 m
15 130 m

C p. 96

1 1232 m **2** 1258 m
3 1581 m **4** 125 m
5 1877 m **6** 4841 m